THE SKILL OF FREEDOM

Book design by Alan Hebel

ISBN: 978-3-9828451-0-4 (Paperback)

First published in 2026

Published by Master Your Path
www.shimritnativ.com

THE SKILL OF FREEDOM

Crack *the* Code *of the*
HUMAN INSTRUMENT®

Shimrit Nativ

Foreword by Neale Donald Walsch

FOREWORD

I wish with all my heart that someone had told me before I was 50 years old, for gosh sake, that the combination of my Body and my Mind is not who I am. I wish someone had told me that I am a *spiritual* entity, *having* a Body and a Mind, and that these were merely instruments—tools, if you will; basically, *equipment*—used by my True Self to serve its agenda. I wish, further, that someone had told me *what that agenda is.*

In short, I wish to high heaven I could have read the book by Shimrit Nativ that you have right in front of you. Well, she hadn't written it yet back then, but she's written it now, and it's a true gift, a remarkable resource, a very real treasure to anyone seeking to not only *understand* more of, but to *make* more of, their life during their time here on Earth.

Ms. Nativ has packed greater amounts of practical insight and powerful illumination regarding the human journey than I have seen in one place in a very long time. This is a book that is truly *helpful* as humans seek to navigate the roadway between birth and death. Yes, I would call it exactly that: a roadmap, showing every life traveler how to get from where they are to where they want to be.

Have a yellow felt-tip pen nearby as you read these pages. You're going to want to highlight sentences and paragraphs galore, I promise you.

—Neale Donald Walsch

"Tempest-tossed souls, wherever you may be, under
whatsoever conditions ye may live, know this —

in the ocean of life the isles of Blessedness are smiling,

and the sunny shore of your ideal awaits your coming.

Keep your hands firmly upon the helm of thought.

In the barque of your soul recline
the commanding Master;

He does but sleep;

wake Him.

Self-control is strength; Right Thought is mastery;
Calmness is power.

Say unto your heart, 'Peace be still!'"

—James Allen

CONTENTS

INTRODUCTION

"Do not allow your life to represent anything but the grandest version of the greatest vision you ever had about Who You Are."

—NEALE DONALD WALSCH

Welcome, beloved.

This book is about **You**.

I remember who you truly are, and this book serves as a Re-Minder—so that you may Re-Member with your Soul and allow its full expression in your Life.

Through these pages, you are invited to create and embody the 'Grandest version of the greatest vision of Who You Truly Are.'

You have been gifted a marvelous tool: the **Human Instrument**. It holds within it the capacity to shape, direct, and experience anything you desire—once you master its skill and **crack its code**.

This book will show you how.

Preparing for Your Journey

To make the most of this experience, I invite you to take a few intentional steps before we begin:

- **Dedicate a Journal:**
  Choose a new journal specifically for this journey. Use it to record your insights, reflections, and notes. It will also serve as a space for the integration exercises included in the upcoming chapters.

- **Access the Book's Meditations:**
  Visit **www.skilloffreedom.com** to access the guided meditations. These meditations are an essential part of the integration process and will support you in embodying the teachings on a deeper level.

Now, as you step into this path of remembrance and transformation—I bless you forth, with love.

Farewell, and Godspeed.

PRELUDE

I chose to come here.
Before form, before name, before body—I was pure, loving awareness.
I was called forth to materialize, to express my essence in the physical world.

And so, I chose You. Beloved You, little one.

I chose your mother and father.
I chose the time of your birth.
I chose your home, your body, your lessons, and your gifts.
I chose your pains and your pleasures.

I laid out a Path for you to unravel and master, so that you may return Home, to Me.

I AM forever calling You.
I AM forever loving You.
I AM forever with You.
I AM the Truth of Who You Are.

Integration

Recall the Truth of who You are - your Soul.

To deepen this remembrance, use the meditation available on **www.skilloffreedom.com**

Then, journal freely.
Repeat this practice daily for seven days, or longer—whenever the call arises.

1

THE FIRST CHOICE

"Begin to see yourself as a soul with a body rather than a body with a soul."

—WAYNE DYER

I chose to be born into a family of four—my mother, father, and two brothers. My birth was difficult. They almost lost this little body, and my visit to this world could have been very brief—but they saved me.

There was a hole in my family, and I came as a gift. My middle brother was born with a severe case of cerebral palsy. For six years, my parents did everything they could to help him improve, but to no avail. He couldn't communicate, swallow on his own, walk, stand, or control his body independently. He was entirely dependent on others for every need.

And then I arrived.

Now, there was a newborn in the house. The doctors had convinced my parents that my brother had no conscious awareness—that his crying, laughter, and reactions were merely chemical reflexes to sounds and light.

Wanting to give me and my older brother the best life possible, my parents made the painful decision to place my middle brother in a specialized home for children like him, so they could devote more time and energy to creating a joyful and balanced environment for my older brother and I to grow up in. I was only six months old when this happened.

For the next five and a half years, we visited my brother every two weeks. I remember those visits vividly. I remember loving my brother and connecting with his Soul—the Truth of who he is.

I would play with him, hold his hands and lift them to his head or shoulders, laugh with him... and then I would leave, returning home with the rest of my family, while he stayed behind.

•

These visits deeply shaped the inner world of that little girl, cultivating feelings of confusion, guilt, and sorrow. The Truth she sensed about her brother's Soul—and her own—was not acknowledged by the adults and the reality around her. This created an internal split, planting seeds of self-doubt, a fear of abandonment, and a deep unconscious need to prove her worth—to ensure she would never have the same destiny as her brother.

But other seeds were planted as well—ones that would later sprout into a passion and a gift: the ability to connect with others on a Soul level, to help them discover and express their Truth, and to break free from limitation and suffering.

•

My brother passed away at the age of twelve. Years later, in my early twenties, during a time of deep self-inquiry and awakening, I was looking through his photo album in my parents' living room when I found his funeral notice. I discovered that he had been buried exactly on my sixth birthday!

In that moment—ready for a change I could no longer ignore—I felt something unmistakable settle into place. Not just a thought or emotion, but a deep inner clarity, as if a hidden agreement within me had finally been activated. I couldn't yet name it, but I sensed the beginning of alignment with a deeper part of myself—a Truth I hadn't known how to listen to until then.

My name is Shimrit Nativ. My middle brother's name was Nitzan. In Hebrew, *Nitzan* means *sprout*, and *Nativ* means *path*. *Shimrit* can be translated as *little keeper*.

So, I chose to be born as the little keeper of the path that sprouted with my beloved brother—who passed to me a precious baton: the remembrance of who I Am in Truth. Of who we all truly are.

To remind **You** of who You Are in Truth.

Integration

Look back as far as you can into your early childhood. Identify the experiences that contributed to your sense of separation. Recognize the events that planted the seeds of your gifts, your passion, and your calling. Notice how they have shaped the path you're here to walk and master—the path leading you to the 'Grandest version of the greatest vision of Who You Truly Are.'

2

THE DESTIN(Y)ATION

Watch your thoughts, for they become your words.
Watch your words, for they become your actions.
Watch your actions, for they become your habits.
Watch your habits, for they become your character.
Watch your character, for it becomes your destiny.

—LAO TZU

You might be feeling like no matter what you do, your life keeps going in circles and no significant change is really possible.

For example: you might be working very hard to improve your financial position and always end up with the same balance at the end of each month.

Perhaps you've been attempting to reach your ideal weight and fitness goals for years, only to repeatedly find yourself back where you started.These cycles might cause you to feel limited and trapped, bound to a destiny that is not by your choice or control.

But the Truth is: Your destiny is **Freedom**. This path you are on leads to a glorious destination—the ultimate goal—the remembering with the Truth of who You Are.

The path is a spiral one, with many turns, beginnings, and endings, winding through cycles of remembering, choosing, and becoming. You are perpetually creating your destiny by directing each cycle, expanding your story with every chapter and every choice.

Some people choose to follow a single destination—a clear trail with a singular trajectory. Every cycle in their spiral mirrors the one before and after. Some fulfill their true destiny of freedom only when they leave the physical body and human self in the cycle we call death—finally becoming Soul in its purest form.

But the Soul is calling you—relentlessly, steadily, persistently, unconditionally—perpetually seeking expression through you.

Like the beam of a lighthouse, it shines consistently, even when your mind is clouded by fog or distracted by waves.

With every new cycle, you're invited to choose a new destination—another level of embodiment, another facet of what Neale Donald Walsch so beautifully called *'The Grandest Version of the Greatest Vision of Who You Are'*—ready to be expressed.

Freedom can be expressed and experienced in many forms. **It is a *skill* that you can practice and master.**

The ultimate freedom, and the only freedom that truly exists, is the freedom to choose your thoughts and focus of attention. With your Human Instrument you have the ability to accept and reject ideas, as well as originate new ones.

Ideas are like spiritual seeds, potential realities you can realise, when mastering the Instrument and Skill of Freedom and deliberate creation.

Answering the call and accepting the sacred assignment to manifest the gift of Life, whether it arrives as an idea, image, or vision, sets a new destination and, potentially, an updated destiny on your path (this will, of course, require you to bring this new vision and version into manifestation through new choices of thoughts, words and actions. This is the reprogramming process and will be discussed and integrated in depth later in this book).

This updating and recalibrating can occur many times throughout the journey.

It's like hiking a vast landscape and spotting a new peak in the distance. The path may shift, but the impulse to move forward remains unchanged.

You can choose a new destination again and again.

In fact, this is the true nature of Life—to ever evolve and expand.

Let me show you how this unfolded in my journey:

Cycle 1

Discovering in my early twenties that my brother was buried on my sixth birthday gave meaning and purpose to my path, fundamentally altering my perception of myself and my destiny. This marked my second great choice (the first one is the birth, as shared in chapter 1)—one that forever changed the course of my journey.

A lifelong Desire to be close to nature had burned within me since childhood. This Desire was amplified by an inner drive to connect with my brother's Soul and a yearning to embody my role as the keeper of the path our bond had sprouted.

This passion led me to a relationship with a man who became my life partner for five years. He lived outdoors, off-grid, and had a son with cerebral palsy. For those five years, I too lived outdoors, chopping wood for fires for cooking and heating water for bucket showers, collecting herbs, growing vegetables, and hunting catfish and ducks with a spear and bow & arrow.

During that time, I became the closest person to his son, caring for him in every possible way, in deep love and connection.

You see, the attention I was directing to the memory and meaning of the early experiences in my life and the Soul-relationship with my brother, coupled with my yearning to be immersed in nature, manifested in this new reality.

However, a lack of awareness regarding how those early experiences shaped my identity and self-image led me to choose a partner who did not support my highest well-being. This turned out to be a self-sabotaging pattern, which I would only manage to shift after great hardship in the years that followed (I'll share that story in a later chapter).

During this period of living outdoors another passion was also awakened: music, specifically the flute. I began teaching myself how to play, discovering sound and melody through exploration and intuition. This started a whole new trajectory, with more cycles and turns in my spiral path.

Cycle 2

Have you ever sensed that a long-held passion wasn't just a hobby, but a signpost pointing to your next chapter?

During those years, music became my primary focus. The Desire to master the flute and the language of music deepened. Eventually, this led me to change direction once again and set a new destination. I left behind the outdoor life to pursue music professionally. At 27, I applied to the Music Academy and became a jazz musician.

This was not an easy choice. It led me to leave behind the life I'd built with my partner and his son, and step into a world of musicians without having any experience of my own. But my Desire to become a professional musician defined my new destination, to which I was devoted.

Three years into this new path, my Soul's calling grew louder. Musical ideas surfaced, and a new voice—my own—emerged. The Desire to express Spirit through this medium intensified, leading me to make yet another choice and shift my trajectory once again.

Cycle 3

I left the university and immersed myself in the search for melodies and words, refining my skills in singing and composing the music that was flowing to and through me.

This choice, again, was not easy. On the outside it looked reckless and irresponsible, to quit my studies for an arcane search. Indeed, the uncertainty was confusing, even scary at times, but I was determined to follow the calling I was hearing from within and find its answer.

This led me to write and record an album, perform internationally, and collaborate with extraordinary musicians.

My musical career unfolded over many years. During this time, I married, became a mother, relocated to a new country, and continued to grow and evolve.

Cycle 4

Have you ever felt compelled to walk away from something you'd mastered, even something you loved, because your Soul was calling you into a greater expression?

By my late thirties, the Desire to support others on their self-actualisation journey, and to serve as a guide and keeper of their path, grew stronger and stronger. This was my lifelong calling which now grew impossible to ignore.

Once again, I made a choice and set a new destination. I left my musical career to follow the guidance of my Soul, devoting myself to study and practice, embodying my purpose as a coach and mentor.

Following this new trajectory, I launched an online business to reach more people and step fully into the leadership I was being called to. I refined my methods and deepened my tools to serve others, playing my part in the evolution of our collective consciousness, one person at a time.

•

Andrew Carnegie once said: *"Any idea that is held in the mind, that is either feared or revered, will begin at once to clothe itself..."*

You can take any idea and bring it into life. You can set any goal, any destination, and choose your destiny.

The only reason you may have experienced failure in doing so is lack of skill over the Human Instrument, and the following chapters will guide you in developing and mastering it.

But first, let's unravel your deeper purpose and anchor in the intention to choose the path that leads to its expression and fulfilment.

Integration

Take a moment to reflect on these questions:

- What are your gifts, with which you can bring value to yourself and others?
- What gifts are still waiting to be discovered and unwrapped?
- What is your purpose in life?
- How willing are you to hear the calling of your Soul, and to answer it?
- Are you ready to change trajectory and set a new destination?

3

THE DESIRE

"Every desire is the effort of an unexpressed possibility to come into action."

—WALLACE D. WATTLES

You may recognize a recurring theme from the previous chapter: **Desire**.

Desire is the voice of your Soul, calling you to bring its essence into form. It is Life seeking expression through you.

On your Royal Path, the True Self guides you through this deep inner signal. When you trust and follow it, you're led toward your greatness—toward your destiny of freedom and abundance—manifesting in the shapes and forms you deeply desire.

Many of us were not taught to honor or follow our desires, or to consider them a leading priority. Often, we were taught the opposite: that desire is selfish, invalid, even dangerous or forbidden.

These beliefs are rooted in fear and misunderstanding.

Following Desire involves the unknown, because you can't truly desire what you already possess. You may feel gratitude for what you have or a wish to sustain it, but that is a different feeling—and a different frequency—than Desire.

Everything is made of the same formless substance: Energy, vibrating at different frequencies. We perceive only what matches the range of our physical senses, but there are countless other frequencies that are just as real, even if we can't detect them.

In other words, we experience what has materialized—what has collapsed and condensed into matter—which we then perceive as our physical reality.

In the quantum field, frequencies and potentials are not separated by space and time as physical objects are. They belong to a unified field of potentiality, from which specific events condense into experience.

Imagine the quantum field like a cloud of unplayed songs.

They're all there—every possibility, every timeline—silent until you tune in. When attention and emotion align with one "song," it begins to play through your life.

The melody you bring into audibility is the experience you live.

The "unknown" is everything in the field that has not yet manifested physically.

Thoughts carry frequency. The moment you think meaningfully about something you Desire, you've tuned to a frequency that already exists in the field.

Your **Human Instrument**—mind, heart, and body—is constantly interacting with that field.

Emotion moves energy. The way you feel reflects the frequency you're running, and your Instrument provides clear feedback through your emotional state.

When you feel a deep Desire, you are attuned to the frequency of that possibility—of your desired reality to manifest. Every frequency in the field is a potential that can condense into physical form when energy is organized and given direction.

Your Human Instrument is doing this all the time.

The Creative Process

Receiving your Desire is like tuning a radio. The song already exists in the airwaves, but you must tune your Instrument precisely to that frequency to hear it. Your thoughts, feelings, and actions are how you tune.

The creative process is constant and unceasing. That is the essence of Life—continuous evolution and expansion. It is the nature of Who You Truly Are.

Your Human Instrument is the perfect vessel for the creative process to unfold through. That is its purpose. However, without conscious awareness, understanding and skill, this marvellous Instrument is used without deliberate intention, often perpetually creating more of the same—or more of what is unwanted—both individually and collectively.

To create something new and desired, you must bring all levels of your Instrument into alignment, allowing the free and complete flow of energy into matter, in harmony with your desired idea.

When you hold a desired idea in thought, you generate a **thought-form**—a frequency in the field. When you feel the Desire deeply, you align your Instrument to that potential and begin moving energy toward **vibrational form** and, ultimately, **physical form**.

It's important to distinguish between Desire and Need, which operate on completely different frequencies.

Need arises from lack, creating contraction, and is ultimately destructive.

Desire arises from expansion and is therefore life-giving.

The next step in the creative process is physical action or movement. In other words, in order to bring your Instrument into full harmony with the frequency of your desired idea—and to allow it to manifest—you must take inspired action that resonates with that Desire.

This, of course, requires Faith.

As we've explored, following Desire meets the unknown, because the thing desired lives there until it's brought through an aligned Instrument in motion.

This is often where the self struggles most: the moment of action. Confronted with uncertainty, the Instrument's default programming shifts into survival, interpreting unfamiliarity as risk and trying to preserve the known.That protective reflex inhibits movement aligned with Desire.

It's like standing at the edge of a cliff, drawn toward something you deeply want on the other side. But as you approach the edge, your old self screams, "Stop, it's not safe!" What you don't yet see is that the next step isn't a fall. It's where the path begins to form beneath your feet. When there is no physical evidence or tangible proof, the mind misreads that absence as a warning sign.

Fear takes the lead.

Instead of stepping into the new, the self retreats into well-worn patterns and familiar behaviors. These may feel safer, but this safety is an illusion—one that often comes at the cost of fulfillment, growth, and truth.

When your attention remains fixed on what has already manifested, you recreate the very same conditions. Your Instrument locks to the current frequency, and the new can't emerge.

I've lived this.

One year into my coaching business, I completely burnt out. I poured all my energy into the mechanical, strategic operations, working harder and harder while sacrificing my spiritual practice, time with my family and my health. I was slowly losing connection to the deeper Desire that had once ignited this path. Instead of tuning into that inner guidance, I found myself focused only on immediate outcomes and external demands.

The burnout hit hard. A severe skin condition emerged—one that left visible scars, which I now carry as lasting reminders of the lesson this experience came to teach me. Eventually, I had to stop everything. I paused my business entirely and turned inward, reconnecting with my Soul and my true Desire.

Burnout is just one example of how being disconnected from your Source of Desire, and from the spiritual essence of reality, is reflected in your experience.

You might also experience emotional pain, financial distress, challenges in relationships, illness and even accidents—they're all symptoms of the same underlying problem.

That healing process brought me back to Source, and with it, the free flow of energy through my Human Instrument. When I relaunched the business, I did so from a completely different frequency. What followed was a quantum leap: the birth of a 7-figure company and a global community, manifested not through striving or stress, but through deep alignment and trust.

A **"Quantum Leap"** is defined as a huge, often sudden,

increase or advance in something. In the context of the personal creative process, it is the transmutation of energy—vibrating at the frequency of a desired potential—into tangible reality.

It's a shift from possibility to embodiment, transcending linear progress.

In essence, it's a "Leap of Faith"—when action is taken in alignment with Desire, with the Soul, and with the unseen but deeply felt—allowing the creative process to unfold through you, transforming possibility into thought-form, then into vibrational form, and finally into physical form—one that can be lived and celebrated.

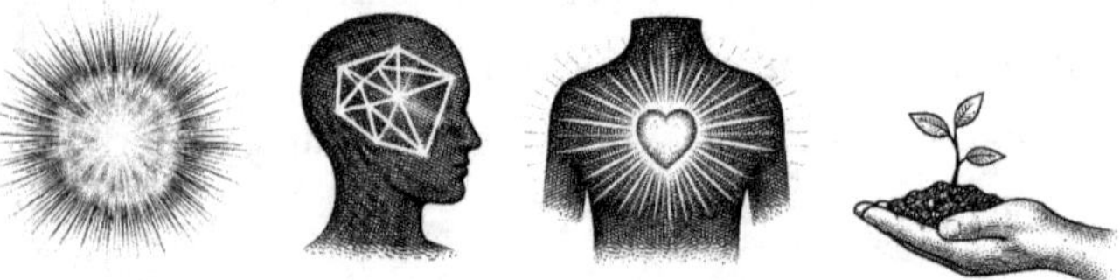

POSSIBILITY ➔ THOUGHT FORM ➔ VIBRATIONAL FORM ➔ PHYSICAL FORM

Every Desire carries a frequency. But without clarity and focus, that frequency can't materialize. Let's explore how to tune your Instrument toward it, through clear, crystallised goals.

Integration

Take your journal and reflect deeply on the following questions. Let each one resonate in your heart and allow your mind to receive the answers as words or images.

Suspend disbelief. You don't need to know how or when.

- What is your Soul's Desire?
- Write everything that comes up: dreams, experiences, and expressions that truly call to you.
- From this place of deep alignment, tune into 'the grandest version of the greatest vision' of yourself.
- Describe in detail how this version of you expresses itself in your life. Use positive words and present tense to affirm its reality.
- Support this process with the guided meditation available on **www.skilloffreedom.com**

Give yourself time and space to explore these questions fully. Let the answers flow freely from within.

4

CRYSTALLISING GOALS

"Goals are for us to grow, not to get."

—BOB PROCTOR

Your marvelous Instrument includes a GPS system that operates much like the map app on your phone. When you set a destination and turn the signal on, it gives you the fastest and easiest directions to get there and automatically recalculates the route each time you go off track. It continues to guide you clearly, as long as the signal stays active.

Quite simply, to use the Instrument efficiently, you must know how to:

1. Set the destination,
2. Turn and keep the signal on, and
3. Follow the directions.

To crystallise a goal through your Human Instrument, you engage three levels:

1. Thought (destination)
2. Emotion (signal)
3. Action (movement)

When these three align, your path becomes clear, and your Instrument functions as the powerful channel it was designed to be.

Imagine you're embarking on a long road trip to a place you've never been, one that takes several days to reach. You'd likely plan to end each day somewhere you can rest for the night, right? You might break it down even more, and plan to reach a certain place where you can have a nice break for lunch.

So, you would enter into your map app your final destination, or perhaps just of the first leg of the journey, along with some key stopovers, allowing the app to suggest the ideal route.

Similarly, you want to crystallise your goals as stepping-stones on the path toward your greater vision. It is important to hold clear in your mind both the final destination of the greatest vision, as well as those crystallised goals on your way there. Without this clarity, you might never move forward, or might never reach your destination, despite your efforts.

Crystallising your goals allows you to focus—and focus increases momentum. It also supports you in building your Faith and climbing the ladder of belief—gradually rising from *hoping* you can fulfill your big vision or dream, to a level of *absolute certainty.*

My late mentor, Bob Proctor, always said, *"Goals are for us to grow, not to get"*. When you set a goal that stretches you beyond where and what you've reached so far, you open the opportunity to grow into the version of yourself who has already reached it. You expand your recognition of yourself to include that expression.

When you set such a goal, you create its thought-form and tune into that frequency that already exists in the field.

And here comes the tricky part.

The frequency of your goal is not the same as the frequency of not having it. As long as you feel like you *must* get there, you won't—because you are not an energetic match to it. Your focus must be on growth and not just achievement.

You can begin to create this expansion and access the frequency of the goal *before* it has manifested in your physical reality. This requires an alignment of your state of being with it.

Your state of being is a composite of your thoughts, feelings, and actions. When these align, you become an energetic match to your goal—allowing energy on that frequency to flow freely from the unified field into your physical reality.

It's like building a bridge across a river.

Your thoughts lay the blueprint. Your feelings pour the foundation. Your actions place the stones. When all three are working together, the path completes, and what once felt out of reach becomes a place you can walk right into.

So, let's tie this back to the GPS system of your Instrument:

When you consciously choose a goal as your next destination, you tune into its frequency with your thought. When you continue thinking in alignment with that goal—from the awareness of it already manifested and awaiting your arrival—you are tuning your Instrument to match this frequency. This enables your actions to be effective in moving you toward the goal, creating and attracting results that are materialized energy on that same frequency.

Think of it as setting a precise destination in your map app and driving your vehicle appropriately. Your thoughts secure the location, your unwavering alignment maintains a strong signal, and your actions propel you forward like wheels steadily advancing toward what awaits at the journey's end.

Your feelings are your GPS signal.

When you feel emotions that are not in alignment with your goal, such as worry, doubt, frustration or fear, you are receiving feedback from your Instrument that you are off track.

In order to get back on the easiest and shortest route to your destination, you must change your frequency and tune it back to that of your Soul & goal.

Emotions are energy in motion, meaning you are moving energy through your Instrument from the non-physical to the physical, according to the frequency you are tuned to at any given moment.

Your Instrument's GPS—the emotional guidance system—gives you a moment-by-moment indication of which frequency you are tuned to, and in which direction you are moving: in the wanted direction that leads to your desired future, or the opposite unwanted trajectory.

The 3 parts of the Human Instrument
S—Spirit ; E—Energy ; M—Mind ; H—Heart ; B—Body

So, your job is to set the destination, align with your Desire, and pay attention to the signals coming from your emotional guidance system—prioritizing your frequency above everything else and choosing thoughts and actions that resonate with your goal.

We will discuss and practice in more depth how to master the skill of tuning your Instrument's frequency, and in fact, we are already well on our way.

Recalling and remembering the Truth of Who You Are, connecting deeply with your Soul's Desire and purpose, and choosing a destination from this level of awareness—already sets a powerful trajectory for your path.

But even as you set your goals and align with their frequency, another force is often at play—the unseen wall within, shaped by early conditioning, that can quietly resist your expansion.

In the next chapter, we'll begin to uncover this inner wall of separation and learn how to open its gates.

Integration

Reconnect with the '*grandest version of the greatest vision of Who You Truly Are*'. From this elevated perspective, identify a steppingstone toward your ultimate vision by looking back to a point in time that would be one year from today. This moment becomes your destination for the next 12 months.

Next, continue to look backward along this timeline from that same higher awareness to a point three months from today. This serves as your shorter-term goal.

Continue mapping out your journey by setting even shorter-term goals in this same way, always in alignment with your vision.

Support this process with the guided meditation available on **www.skilloffreedom.com**

5

THE WALL OF SEPARATION

"And the children struggled within her, and the Lord said unto her, two nations are in thy womb, and two manner of people shall be separated from thy bowels; And the one people shall be stronger than the other people; And the elder shall serve the younger."

—GENESIS 25:22-23

Who you are in Truth is a Soul—a Divine Being, an individuation of Spirit, the Most-High Self.

And then there is the second self: the Human Self, with its mind and body, its needs and wants, pains and pleasures.

This path is one of self-actualisation: expressing the True Self through the Human Self. But between the two, there often stands a wall: subtle, invisible, yet deeply felt, formed early in life, shaped by the illusion of separation, and reinforced by fear and conditioning.

As you walk this path, you begin to unlock gates in that wall, one by one.

And with each opening, more of the Divine Light can shine through your physical experience, actualizing and materializing Spirit in the 3-dimensional plane of physical reality.

Separation from what?

Separation from Oneness. From Spirit. From God. From Energy—call it whatever you will. Separation from the Unity that you are part of.

Coming into this body and environment, which you chose and received as a baby, the Human Instrument you were given went through the conditioning process.

With your Instrument you create and experience Life. It is always in motion, constantly interacting with reality through a cyclic process:

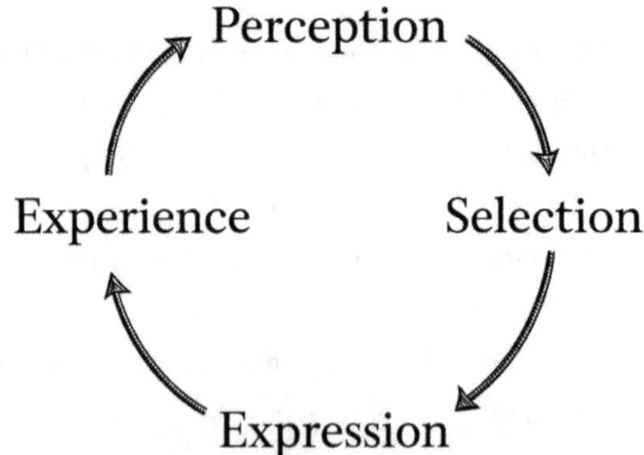

With every cycle, you perceive your reality, select a conception (consciously or unconsciously), express that selection through thoughts, words, and actions—and then experience the result. This loop is how creation flows to and through you.

This marvelous Instrument operates on a program that allows it to perform countless functions and process vast amounts of information continuously. Without conscious awareness, this cycle runs on autopilot.

But as you become aware of it, you begin to reclaim the ability to direct the process—perceiving, choosing, and experiencing in alignment with Who You Truly Are.

This is what true ***Freedom*** is: the freedom to make those selections, choosing how you perceive, express and experience Life.

And this Freedom is a Skill you can practice and master!

We will explore this process and the programming of your Instrument more deeply later in the book. For now, understand that the human-self part of you is this marvellous Instrument—one that has been shaped and conditioned since the moment you entered this physical life.

From the very beginning of your journey in this body, this wall of separation was erected, and has remained in place. Yet the Truth of Who You Are is always calling you to open more and more gates in that wall, so you can remember your Truth and reunite with your True Self—your Soul.

The conditions you experience in life are not random—they reflect the internal programming your Human Self has absorbed over time. In the next chapter I will share a personal story that will give you a vivid example of this process.

This programming is made up of a complex web of beliefs, emotional imprints, patterns of thought, concepts and habitual ways of relating to the world. Your physical reality is like a canvas, painted by the patterns held within, often unconsciously, shaping what unfolds around you.

In the following pages, we'll explore how each of these patterns, challenges, and turning points in your life are not obstacles—but gates: sacred entry points encoded with the lessons your Soul chose for this journey, and serve as the keys to dissolving the wall of separation, one layer at a time.

Integration

Reflect on patterns in your life—areas where you feel stuck in a cycle. It may show up in your body, your health, relationships, money, or elsewhere.

List as many of these patterns as you can identify.

You'll return to this list later in the book and be guided through a process to shift them, one by one.

6

GATES & LESSONS

"A memory without the emotional charge is called wisdom."

—DR. JOE DISPENZA

The recurring cycles in your life, which you identified in the previous chapter, stem from deeply embedded imprints within your Instrument's programming. These patterns were installed through some painful experiences that disconnected you from the knowing of Who You Truly Are.

Every gate in the wall of separation guards not just pain, but a lesson, a key, and the potential for expansion and freedom.

Ever since you were born, in order to adapt to your physical environment and emotionally survive in it, you unconsciously selected reactions that helped you feel safe, balanced, and validated by others.

These responses became familiar, even automatic, like an inner script designed to protect you.

For example, if as a child you learned that being quiet and agreeable earned approval, while expressing strong emotions led to conflict or disconnection, you may have shaped your behavior to stay small and keep the peace. Later in life, without realizing it, you might still default to holding back your Truth.

As long as you continue to perceive reality through that original pattern and react in the same way, you'll continue to express life through that filter, recreating the same course, and generating the same outcomes.

Every time you notice a cycle repeating in your life, it is an invitation to update to change the pattern in which the creative process is moving through you, make a new selection, one that leads to an upgraded expression and experience.

By doing this you are rewriting the script and overriding the old, outdated pattern. Each such cycle of the old pattern that appears in your life is a knock on one of the gates in your wall of separation, calling you to choose differently.

This is where your emotional GPS becomes essential. When a pattern resurfaces, along with familiar feelings such as frustration, sadness, or shame, your Instrument is sending you clear feedback. It reveals where you've veered off the true course of your Soul's Desire.

Remember: When a pattern reappears—it's a signal. Your emotional GPS alerts you that you're standing at a familiar threshold.

It's an opening to shift your selection and interrupt the old cycle. That new selection leads to a new expression.

And that new expression creates a new experience—one that reflects your Soul's true Desire.

Each time you make that new choice, you open another gate in the wall of separation, allowing more of your Divine Light to move into form.

Every new choice is a sacred practice of the Skill of Freedom.

Those early life events, and the repeating cycles they triggered, hold wisdom waiting to be unlocked. By accessing that wisdom, you expand your awareness and transform your expression and experience.

As long as you continue to repeat the cycle of perceiving → selecting → expressing → experiencing life through a pattern formed in pain, you cannot access the wisdom and break through.

But the moment you release the emotional charge and observe your reality with detachment and awareness, you unlock the wisdom within the lesson and open a gate in your wall of separation, that leads to an expanded experience of life.

In Hebrew, the words for “lesson” and “gate” share the same three-letter root (ש.ע.ר), and the word for “richness” (ע.ש.ר) is a reversal of that root. A powerful Truth is captured and revealed in this:

When you hear the knock and receive the lesson, the gate opens, granting you access to greater expansion, abundance, and richness in life.

Every time you open another gate, more of the Divine Light of Who You Truly Are can shine through your Instrument, projecting the forms of your Desire onto the screen of your reality.

Every time you open a gate, you reclaim more of your power to consciously create and love freely. In the next chapters, we'll begin exploring how to use this reclaimed energy to rewrite the internal blueprint that shapes your reality.

A Personal Example

When I was around 29 years old, I was coming out of yet another relationship. I was already recovering from the heartbreak and settling into a small studio apartment in Jerusalem.

I clearly recognized the pattern, this being my fourth long-term relationship. Yet, I found myself falling in love again with someone who, once more, could not meet my deepest needs and desires, witnessing myself stepping into the same cycle once again, unable to make a new choice.

Again, I took on the futile role of the one who would rescue and transform the man I loved. I believed that if I could help him heal his inner child, he would finally be able to love deeply, and we could live happily ever after (sound familiar?).

Even though I was aware of the pattern, I couldn't break it. My Human Instrument Self was still operating on its automatic program, and I hadn't yet developed the tools to stop and recalibrate it.

At that time, I also began to feel that something wasn't right in my lower abdomen. Looking back, I now know that the knock on my gate was getting louder. My Soul was calling me to unlock the lesson, sending signals through my body to guide me into healing and transformation.

During a checkup, I was diagnosed with an advanced stage of pre-cancerous lesions in my cervix. The doctor advised me to undergo a procedure as soon as possible.

That was the loud enough knock, and this time I was ready to listen, learn and open the gate.

I knew that if I addressed it only on the physical level, I would miss the deeper opportunity: to learn the lesson and release the emotional pain manifesting in my body.

So, I asked for time. I found a doctor who was willing to wait three months while I embarked on an inner healing journey.

I sought guidance from mentors and healers. Through practices, tools, and deep inquiry, I uncovered the pattern that was rooted in early childhood, and that had shaped not only my relationships, but now my physical health.

In the process, I experienced profound forgiveness. I released pain, fear, and shame that had long been held in my emotional and physical body. This liberated arcane wisdom and energy that had been locked in my body, consumed through the survival mode my Instrument was operating on all these years, with patterns of unworthiness, guilt, and fear of abandonment.

With that energy now freed, I redirected it toward healing and creation.

In just a few weeks, my body was healed. I also manifested a relationship with a man who was unlike any I had ever dated. A year later, he became the father of my son, and we are now celebrating 15 years of marriage and counting.

That lesson had been knocking for years. My Soul's quiet, loving voice echoed through every heartbreak, moment of shame, or loneliness. It consistently reminded me of the ever-widening gap I created each time I compromised or forgot my Truth.

Finally, I heard the call and answered.

And when I did, expansion followed. The light of my Soul flowed through the open gate and manifested my Desire for a deep, loving partnership, in a higher expression of myself.

I am forever grateful for the lesson, and for my Soul, which never stopped calling me home to freedom.

While this healing was profoundly transformative, I later uncovered an even deeper wound, one that underpins all others. In the forthcoming chapter, we journey to the very core of separation: the Primal Wound.

Integration

Choose one of the patterns you listed in Chapter 5 and identify a specific situation where this pattern has shown up.

Break it down:

- What are your thoughts, feelings, and behaviors in this situation?
- What in this external experience triggers your reaction?

Now tune into your past, especially your early years, and ask:

- What experiences disconnected you from the Truth of Who You Are?
- What fear, pain, or limiting belief was created within your Human Self?

For each experience, ask:

- What lesson or wisdom would you access if you removed the emotional charge?

Now envision the version of yourself who has already released this pattern and lives in alignment with the lesson.

Break it down:

- What are your thoughts, feelings, and behaviors now—in the same type of situation?

Hold this upgraded version of yourself close. It already exists within you, ready to be chosen.

7

THE PRIMAL WOUND

"I wish I could show you, when you are lonely or in darkness, the astonishing Light of your own Being!"

—HAFIZ

It's remarkable how often, whether clearing layers of conditioning in myself or supporting others in their healing and transformation, I arrive at the same core belief: *"I'm not good enough."* No matter what the outer or inner pattern appears to be, it almost always points back to this.

The self-actualisation journey is a spiral one, and every time we unclothe the self and shed those layers one by one, we get to expand and evolve into a new Desire, when the old costume no longer fits our greatness.

Picture this journey not as a straight line, but as a spiral staircase.

Each turn invites you to meet the same core pain with deeper awareness and greater choice than before.

Each time, it's like peeling back another layer covering the same primal wound, blocking the light of Who You

Truly Are from fully shining through.

For a long time, I believed my core wound stemmed from my early experiences with my brother, who died when I was 6 years old, and from growing up with the experience of his life and death in those first years of my life.

Every transformation cycle I went through: feeling the knock → learning the lesson → opening the gate → stepping into a new level of expansion—seemed to trace back to that old pain.

But then I discovered a deeper Truth: *The core wound isn't in the story!*

You see, even those early experiences with my brother are still just a story—another layer of my self's costume, part of the spiral—and not the core wound itself.

The root of the pain is at the base of that spiral, underneath all those layers, and is what is blocking the Human Self from fully aligning with the Divine Self.

The primal wound is Separation itself. No story. No identity. No personality. Just the illusion of disconnection.

Let me explain.

When you were born into your baby-physical body, you were closer to pure spiritual energy than ever. Unconsciously, you *knew* the Truth of Who You Are.

I say "unconsciously" because as a baby, you didn't yet have conscious awareness. You were in a state of *pure Loving-Awareness*, which is your True Nature, and you did not yet have conscious thoughts and concepts of it, of yourself, or of anything else.

At that early stage, you didn't yet have a cognitive filter to question or interpret what was happening to and around you.

Your subconscious mind was wide open, taking in everything: impressions, suggestions, emotional tones, and unspoken messages from your environment.

These early experiences linked what was happening around you with how you felt inside, creating the first layers of programming in your Human Instrument operating system.

And here is the hidden dissolution:

Most of those external impressions, which came from your caregivers and environment, likely failed to affirm your innate knowing of your Divine Nature.

Instead, they probably communicated the opposite.

Thus, the illusion of separation was born.

Separation from what? (you might ask again)

Separation from Truth.
From Source.
From the Divine Loving-Awareness You Are.

At the base of the spiritual spiral lies this primal wound—**Separation**, entangled with the instinctual need to survive in the physical world.

As a baby-human-self, you had to survive in the environment you were born into and adapt to those around you: their concepts, perceptions, beliefs, expectations, and demands. You needed their approval, acceptance, protection and validation.

And because the world around you didn't reflect the Truth of your pure spiritual nature, that Truth was quickly buried.

This intensified the subconscious programming that shaped your personality, preferences, and narratives. Rooted in that primal wound, it left you feeling separate and misunderstood, as if the Truth you held had no place or acknowledgment in your surrounding reality.

And so, a deep and unspoken belief formed: *"There must be something wrong with me."*

That inherent knowingness and Desire for unconditional love and acceptance was masked by feelings of unworthiness to receive it, or with conditioning around what was expected of you in order to earn something that *resembled* pure love and acceptance but was filtered through learned expectations. This formed concept was so different from the unconditional Love you once unconsciously knew.

This is how the layers began to accumulate, clothing the Divine Self in the story of your human experiences and conditions. Layer upon layer added echelons to the core primal wound, manifesting in circumstances, reflecting in relationships, and projecting patterns onto your physical body and personality.

From then onwards, every time you were told to "be realistic" when sharing your fantasies and dreams, every time you were told to tone down your excitement or dim down your light in any way, every time you were unseen or misunderstood, every time you had to shut down your passion or creativity and fit in... All those experiences created more and more layers in the spiral, more and more bricks in the wall of separation.

All the stories, all the patterns, all the emotional imprints, layer upon layer, they all trace back to the **same core illusion**:

That we are separate from Love.
Separate from Source.
Separate from our True Self.

Dissolving that illusion isn't *part* of the journey.

It *is* the journey.

The ultimate work is to heal that primal wound of separation.

To *re-member* the Truth of our worthiness.
To reclaim the Light of our own Being.

So, I ask you now:
Are you up for the task?

Integration

Support this process with the guided meditation available on **www.skilloffreedom.com**

8

THE PROGRAMMING PROCESS

"It is no exaggeration to say that every human being is hypnotized to some extent either by ideas he has uncritically accepted from others, or ideas he has repeated to himself or convinced himself are true."

—DR. MAXWELL MALTZ

If you're here in Chapter 8, I trust your answer to the previous question was yes.

Yes to the task.
Yes to remembering who You Are.
Yes to healing the primal wound.

Yes to cracking the code of the Human Instrument and mastering the Skill of Freedom.

Now, it's time to explore how the patterns of the subconscious program were formed, so you can begin to dissolve them and reclaim your royal path.

To reach and heal the core wound of separation, we must gently begin peeling back the layers that have concealed the True Self. These layers were added along the spiral path through the programming process—a process that began the moment your Soul entered the physical dimension through your mother's womb.

While a small portion of this programming is genetic, the vast majority stems from environmental input. We now know that even gene expression can be influenced and altered, which means the genetic blueprint can also be updated or deactivated.

Environmental conditioning includes everything you heard, saw, sensed, felt, and perceived from your earliest moments. All of it was, and still is, stored in the neuro-circuitry of your brain, on a subconscious level.

The Programming Process

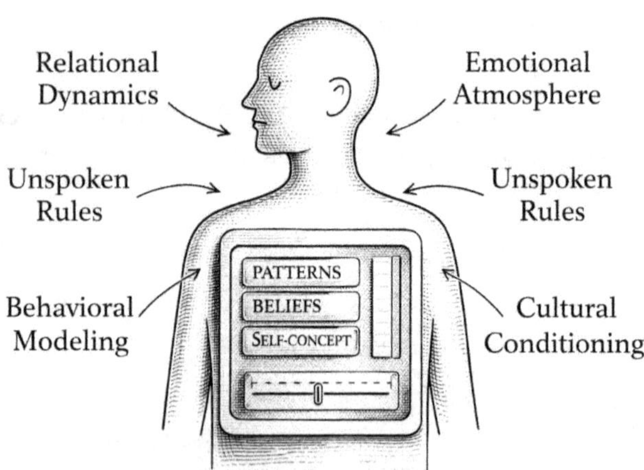

In other words, your magnificent Human Instrument, designed to guide you toward any destination you choose, has been operating on a program that was set during the earliest years of your life. And that inner structure continues to shape your experience according to those early settings that matched the reality of your childhood, unless it is intentionally updated.

The Subconscious Operating System

Your Human Instrument runs on patterns formed long before you could choose them. It is programmable. The internal setting it operates on today was created through the beliefs, experiences, and frequencies that surrounded you, especially in the first 7 formative years of your life, when your subconscious mind was wide open and unfiltered.

This program functions similarly to an autopilot system. Your "plane" has the ability to fly anywhere, with unlimited supply of energy, but the course is preset. If you deviate from that course, the autopilot is automatically activated to return you to the programmed path, leading you to the same destination repeatedly, regardless of your conscious desires or efforts.

This is why patterns and experiences can seem to repeat themselves and why even hard work and intention sometimes don't seem to change your results and lead to new destinations.

The story I shared earlier about burning out in my first year of business is a powerful example of how this plays out in real life.

Because I was operating on an outdated subconscious pattern that didn't match my new chosen destiny I had set (leading a successful global business), the autopilot of my Instrument kicked in and led me right back to zero: no business, no revenue, and no ability to create the impact I was called to make.

It wasn't until I went deep into the operating system of my Instrument and consciously rewrote the program, updating its settings to align with my true destination, that I was able to set a new course and begin moving forward in the desired direction in a sustainable way, creating a lasting change inside and out.

Externally, that translated into restarting my business, rebuilding my team, re-engaging my clientele, and establishing the platforms through which I could share my message and mission. It also meant finally allowing myself to receive and circulate the financial prosperity I had previously been unconsciously blocking.

Dr. Maxwell Maltz called this system a "Psychocybernetic Mechanism": an automatic, self-correcting program, similar to a thermostat or autopilot, that always brings you back to a preset point or level.

In the book *The Big Leap*, Gay Hendricks describes a similar idea with the term "The Upper Limit":

> "The Upper Limit Problem is our universal human tendency to sabotage ourselves when we have exceeded the artificial upper limit we have placed on ourselves. The Upper Limit Problem is caused by a too-low thermostat setting on our ability to achieve and enjoy our ultimate success."

This upper limit is the result of subconscious programming—an inner setting that defines how much success, joy, freedom, or love you're "allowed" to experience before you unconsciously pull yourself back.

The Biology of Programming

Let's explore the biological side of how this programming takes hold.

The human brain operates in several different brainwave frequencies: Delta, Theta, Alpha, Beta, and Gamma.

- **Gamma:** The fastest neural oscillations, associated with high-level cognitive functioning, memory binding, focus, and consciousness.
- **Beta**: Characterized by active thought, alertness, and concentrated mental engagement (likely the state you are in right now as you read).
- **Alpha**: The relaxed state between waking and sleeping—associated with light, meditation and creativity.
- **Theta**: The state of deep meditation, dreaming, and hypnosis.
- **Delta**: Deep, dreamless sleep.

GAMMA WAVES	HIGH-LEVEL COGNITIVE FUNCTIONING HEIGHTENED FOCUS CONSCIOUSNESS
BETA WAVES	ALERTNESS CONCENTRATION THINKING
ALPHA WAVES	VISUALIZATION TRANCE DREAMING
THETA WAVES	DEEP MEDITATION CREATIVITY RELAXATION
DELTA WAVES	DEEP SLEEP TRANSCENDENCE RESTORATION

As you can see, in the range between Alpha and Delta, your body is relaxed or completely still, and your conscious mind is either unfocused or entirely off. These brain waves are therefore associated with unconscious and subconscious states or levels of mind.

When the brain is in Alpha or Theta states, like while dreaming, or when in a deep meditative state, or even while being immersed in a watching a film, the body often responds as if the imagined scene is physically real. This is because, in those moments, the body is being directed not by the conscious mind, but by subconscious conditioning.

During the first 7—12 years of life, your brain operated mostly in Theta and Alpha waves, leaving your subconscious wide open to every impression from your environment.

HUMAN BRAIN WAVES by AGE

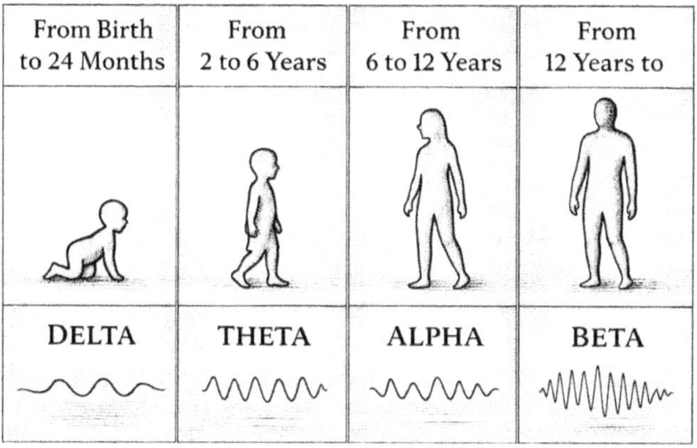

From Birth to 24 Months	From 2 to 6 Years	From 6 to 12 Years	From 12 Years to
DELTA	THETA	ALPHA	BETA

This served your survival and development as a human in that environment, allowing you to learn countless functions and embed vast amounts of information directly into the operating system of your Instrument. As a result, you were quickly able to automatically perform basic and complex actions, like holding objects, walking, and speaking, without needing to consciously think about how to perform them.

Alongside these physical skills, you also absorbed emotional responses, behavioral patterns, cultural cues, and beliefs about yourself and the world—all imprinted into your subconscious, without your judgment or resistance.

In your early years, these served an important purpose: they helped you *emotionally* adapt and survive in your environment.

However, as an adult, these same imprints now form the subconscious program that *limits your ability to change.*

For example, during those formative years, you may have learned to lower your expectations about what was possible for you. You might have been conditioned to abandon your dreams, desires, or beliefs in order to avoid feeling disappointed, ridiculed, or misunderstood.

Through repeated impressions and interactions, while being in a hypnotic state due to the brainwaves your brain was operating on at the time, this conditioning has set your inner thermostat to a certain Upper Limit regarding what you expect and believe you can create and enjoy in life.

But here's the key: that internal setting isn't fixed. Like any system, it can be recalibrated. This takes awareness, intention, and practice, and **it is a central and essential aspect of the Skill of Freedom.**

As long as you do not know how to update the program your Human Instrument is operating on, you can never be free to create and experience life as you desire, and will forever be bound to the course that's been set before you had the ability to choose it.

This program is the code of your Human Instrument, and when you know how to unlock and rewrite it you are mastering the Instrument and the skill.

So, let's continue exploring this system in action:

The subconscious program is a multitude of those patterns, beliefs, and habits that shape your concept of yourself and reality. You've learned to accept some things without question, while doubting others, based entirely on the dominant beliefs of your environment during those early years.

For example, you were taught about the law of gravity. Even though you cannot see, hear, or touch it, you accept its certainty without question. You instinctively avoid actions that would endanger your physical survival, such as stepping out of a high building's window, without needing conscious thought to follow that course of action.

However, this automatic response was not always in place. At a young age, your safety relied on the conscious awareness of the adults around you, their warnings and directions. Only when you were old enough, and, in other words, programmed enough, did this behavior become an automatic part of your subconscious.

Yet, there are other universal laws that your environment may have been unaware of, and therefore, did not imprint into your subconscious and understanding. One such example is the Law of Vibration and Attraction, which decrees that everything vibrates, and that physical reality manifests according to how frequencies match and materialize.

So, even if you are now already aware of this law and understand intellectually that the real cause of everything you experience is your vibration and the internal state of being—even if you mentally accept these concepts as true—you might not yet embody them. You may still need to apply conscious effort in order to operate in accordance with them in ways that support your wellbeing rather than the opposite.

Freedom and prosperity are skills you can practice and master.

Your subconscious program dictates over 95% of your thoughts, feelings, and actions. When you update this programming, your internal operations—thoughts, feelings, and actions—will automatically align with the frequency of what you wish to create and experience physically. The universal laws will then respond with absolute certainty, just as they do when your internal state aligns with the absence of what you desire.

We'll deepen our learning of this skill in the chapters to come. For now, begin applying what you've discovered about your programming, by consciously updating your inner settings to match your desired destination.

Integration

Go back to the pattern you began shifting in Chapter 6.

Revisit Step 5 of that process and now articulate 1—5 statements that reflect the new version of yourself—your upgraded thoughts, feelings, and actions.

Then, support this process with the guided meditation available on **www.skilloffreedom.com**

Practice entering a relaxed, receptive state and impress these affirmations into your subconscious.

Repetition creates new programming. You're now becoming the conscious creator of your own operating system.

9

ROOTS OF CREATION

"Faith doesn't question. Faith knows."

—NEVILLE GODDARD

A significant aspect of our shared human subconscious programming is the conditioning to prioritize information received through our five physical senses. While this was crucial for physical survival, it can also restrict our capacity to create an upgraded life experience.

Survival and Creation are polar opposites.

To survive, you must re-act to perceived or potential danger. This requires you to fixate on the external environment and forecast the future based on past experiences and worst-case scenarios—so you can survive them. In this re-active state, your brain typically operates on heightened beta brainwaves, and you often feel anxious or stressed.

Both desired best-case scenario and feared worst-case scenario already exist as a non-physical reality in the unified field.

In this state of survival, you're not tuning your frequency to what you desire, but to what you fear.

By directing your attention to the external world, to what has already happened and based on that try to predict what might happen, you divert energy away from the potentiality of your Desire and direct it to the very thing you fear or resent.

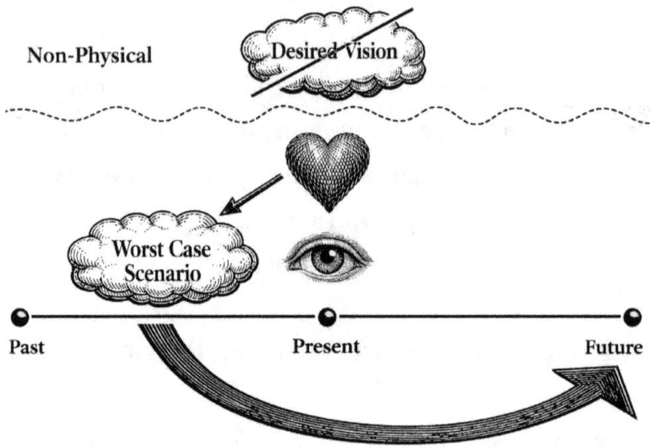

In Hebrew, the phrase "to pay attention" is translated as "to put your heart."

When you give your heart to what you fear or worry, you circulate your vital creative energy toward those possibilities, amplifying them with your focused attention.

Biologically, in these states, your brain operates in Beta brainwave frequencies associated with heightened alertness and problem-solving, as well as with a state of stress and anxiety.

In this state, you cannot tune in to the frequency of your desired future and cannot access the field of infinite possibilities, nor the deeper subconscious layers where transformation occurs.

Instead, you're reinforcing the familiar, recreating the past rather than allowing the unknown to take form. You re-act, meaning repeat past actions, and produce the same familiar results, instead of choosing new ways to reach new destinations.

But what if you were to connect emotionally and mentally with the reality of your unmanifested Desire *in the present moment*, and start living from that envisioned reality?

When you do, your future becomes a reflection of it and no longer a repetition of what has been, but a conscious creation of what can be.

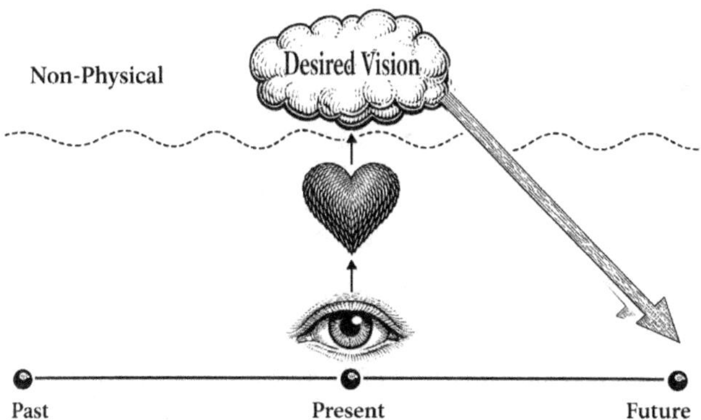

To create something new and desired, you must focus your attention on what you want that has not yet manifested physically. You must think, feel, and act, *knowing* it is as, or even more real, as your current physical reality.

Only then can it take form through the universal laws you've come to understand and embody.

This is the level of mastery: the practice of deliberate creation, *the Skill of Freedom and prosperity.*

And yes, as we said, this requires **Faith**.

One of my favorite quotes from Bob Proctor is:

> "Faith and fear both demand that we believe in something that hasn't yet happened."

Words are capsules of energy.

We have already seen how **create** and **react** are energetic opposites, acting as mirror reflections in both their spelling and their fundamental nature. While one is a deliberate action for shaping reality, the other is a survival mechanism—a pattern rooted in the past.

We also looked at the words **Faith** and **fear**.

In Hebrew, my native language, many words share roots that reveal hidden connections and deeper truths.

The word "fear" in Hebrew is written פ ח ד. Its reversed form, ד ח פ, means "impulse." The impulse is the guidance coming from your Soul, to move past the fear.

When followed with action, it leads to the unfolding manifestation of your Desire. And of course, again, to follow that impulse and move past the fear, Faith is required.

In Hebrew, the word "Faith" comes from the root א מ ן, which is the universal word of prayer and thanksgiving—**Amen.** Other words in Hebrew that come from this same root are Trust, Belief, Practice, Art, Devotion, and Mastery.

Can you see the depth of wisdom this reveals?

> "Faith is the substance of things hoped for, the evidence of things unseen."
>
> *Hebrews 11:1*

The art of creation is all about mastering the skill of living in Faith, fully trusting and believing the unseen, the Truth of Who You Are, the unknown.

And just like any skill, it requires devoted practice of the Skill of Freedom and art of creation.

Moreover, In Hebrew, the word "creation" shares the same root as "Desire" and "impulse"—all pointing to the Soul's essence reaching toward expression.

Addiction to the Known

Now let's consider the word **"Unknown"**—the place where all creation begins, and the realm you must access through Faith.

In Hebrew, "unknown" shares its root with the word "addiction."

We are, in a very real way, addicted to the familiar.

On a biological level, dominant thought patterns activate specific neural pathways, which trigger corresponding chemicals in the brain and body. Most of our repetitive thoughts are fear-based, focused on external threats and stressors. These thoughts trigger addictive stress chemicals, causing the body to "crave" the familiar tension of the survival-mode.

Over time, the body becomes chemically conditioned to feelings like fear, worry, or anxiety, even though these feelings are unpleasant.

This is one reason why it can feel so hard to change.

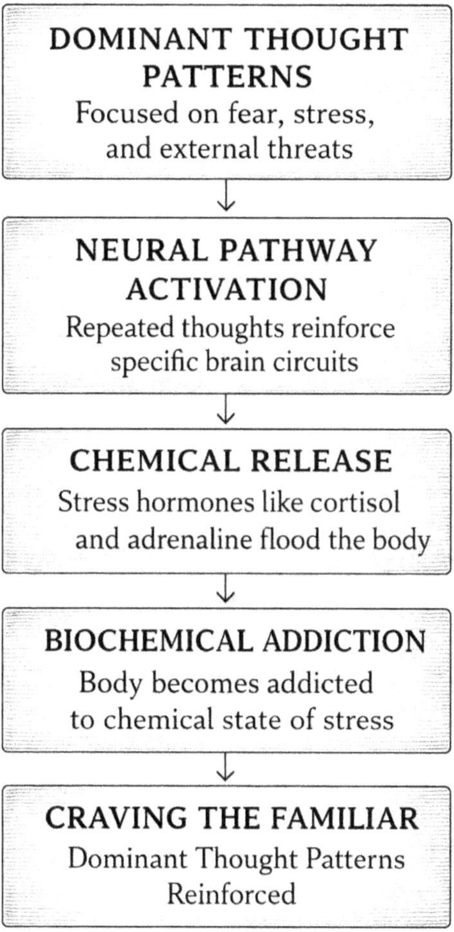

DOMINANT THOUGHT PATTERNS
Focused on fear, stress, and external threats

↓

NEURAL PATHWAY ACTIVATION
Repeated thoughts reinforce specific brain circuits

↓

CHEMICAL RELEASE
Stress hormones like cortisol and adrenaline flood the body

↓

BIOCHEMICAL ADDICTION
Body becomes addicted to chemical state of stress

↓

CRAVING THE FAMILIAR
Dominant Thought Patterns Reinforced

Let's see how this might show up in real life:

You want more peace, but your body is wired for urgency—so when things quiet down, you unconsciously stir drama just to feel normal.

You dream of expansion, but your nervous system only knows how to operate in survival—so growth feels unfamiliar and scary.

You crave financial freedom, but your system is conditioned to the tension of "just enough"—so ease feels unearned, and abundance slips through.

You long to lead with clarity and vision, but your body is hooked on over-efforting—so rest feels like weakness.

You CAN

Now, we understand more deeply what it means to **master the Human Instrument**.

In Hebrew, the word "Instrument" is the inversion of the word "can."

When you awaken the Master within and consciously use and direct your Instrument, you *can* experience the life you desire, and express Who You Are in Truth, in an ever-expanding path of creation.

Your Human Instrument is a vessel for *moving energy*. In the next chapter, we'll explore how to direct that motion with precision and intention.

Integration

Reflect and journal:

- In what areas of your life are you operating from survival, rather than creation?
- What impulses have you ignored due to fear or doubt?
- Where do you feel addicted to the familiar?
- What would it look like to respond to your next Soul impulse with Faith instead of fear?

Then, return to your statements from Chapter 8.

Repeat them while in a calm, receptive state—knowing that every repetition is an act of rewiring and recalibration.

10

MOVING ENERGY

"My mind is a center of divine operation that is always for expansion and fuller expression of something entirely new."

—THOMAS TROWARD

By the Law of Perpetual Transmutation of Energy, energy is always moving into form.

Read this:
You are a center of distribution of energy. You direct energy into forms you create with your Human Instrument. (Now read it again.)

As already explored, emotions are energy in motion. This means that the energy that is flowing to and through you in any and every given moment is moving in a direction assigned to it by how you *feel*. Your awareness of how you feel also gives you an indication of the direction in which you are moving the energy.

Most people move energy unconsciously, reacting emotionally to experiences rather than choosing and directing them. We often say, "I feel X because of Y," but this is a fundamental error. In Truth, the cause of your experience is always how you feel, and not vice versa.

Emerson called the *Law of Cause and Effect* “the law of laws.” How you move the energy is the cause, and your experience is the form the energy has moved into—as the effect.

Understanding this law and how to operate in accord with it consciously and deliberately is the essence of the skill. You are a creator and have at your disposal the most powerful Instrument to create with—your Human Instrument.

Emotions are creative, but as long as you are reacting emotionally by default, you are giving up your creative power and potential.

All matter is made of energy, and energy naturally moves in waves. Even the solid objects we perceive as fixed and physical are, at their core, energetic wave-forms that have collapsed into physical form.

Your emotions set that energy in motion, charging the field with a specific frequency.

What we experience as physical reality is energy—shaped and stabilized through a subtle, often unconscious process, one that reflects the extraordinary power of your emotional state and the direction you assign to your attention.

This leads us to one of the most profound discoveries in quantum mechanics: **The Observer Effect**, which explains how energy responds to awareness and collapses into form.

One of the most famous demonstrations of this is the *Double Slit Experiment.* It demonstrates that subatomic particles behave differently when observed. Without observation, they behave as waves—existing in multiple potential states simultaneously. But when measured or watched, they collapse into a fixed location and behave like matter.

THE DOUBLE-SLIT EXPERIMENT

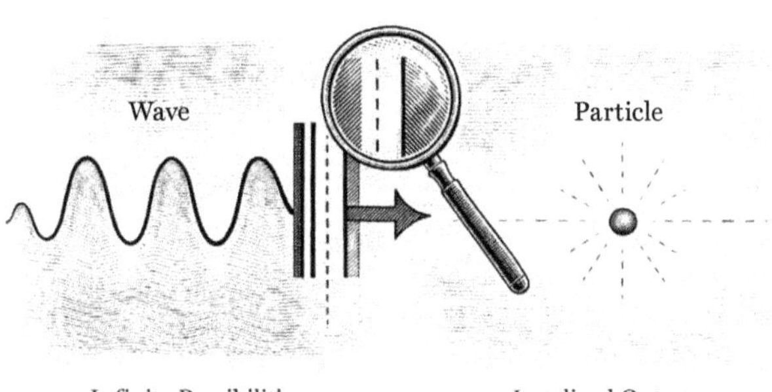

Particles and waves, matter and energy.

This indicates that in the absence of an observer, matter exists only as potential energy. Observation is what causes energy to collapse into form. You collapse possibility into reality by giving it attention. This isn't just a metaphor—it's a fundamental quantum law!

Now, think of energy as water.

Just like a wave is not separate from the ocean, each frequency is not separate from the one energy—the formless substance from which all things are made.

What you observe, you influence. What you focus on, you bring into form.

In the physical world, everything is experienced as matter. Objects appear separate despite being parts of the same environment. Even the cells of your body, though made of energy and information, are perceived as separate.

Science has shown that the atoms, composing everything in the material world, are 99.9999999% energy, or empty space. This "space" is actually filled with quantum fields and active, probabilistic wavefunctions, rather than true nothingness.

Yet human perception is conditioned to experience the material world as composed only of distinct, separate objects.

The Observer Effect

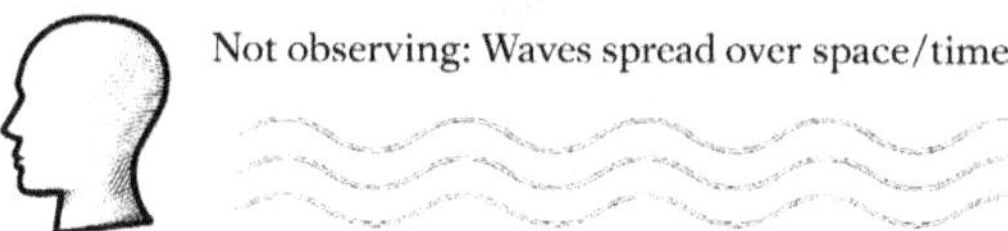

Observing: Particle localised in space/time

Despite knowing that the space between objects is not empty, it is not fully grasped. The deep subconscious programming passed down through generations reinforces the experience of separation.

As we discussed previously, in the first years of your life you had to absorb information from your environment to function as a human in the physical world. This learning wasn't just intellectual, it was imprinted on your subconscious through repetition, emotion, and energetic resonance.

Your self-concept—the image you hold of who you are—was formed through the words, reactions, beliefs, and emotional climate you were immersed in.

It's like a garden being seeded.

Every interaction planted something—an idea, a belief, a story. And over time, those seeds took root. Some grew wild and unchecked. Others were reinforced again and again until they became the dominant landscape of your inner world.

The self-image programmed into your subconscious is what shapes the substance of consciousness into your lived reality. What you harvest in life often grows from the seeds that were planted long before you were aware or able to choose differently.

In order to change your reality, you must change that concept or image of yourself.

> "According to Heisenberg's uncertainty principle, we never know where the electron is going to appear in the electron cloud, yet from nothing comes something. This is why quantum physics is so exciting and unpredictable. The electron is not always physical matter, rather it exists as the energy or is the probability of a wave. It is only through the act of observation by an observer that it appears. Once an observer (mind) comes along and looks for it, the act of observation directs the energy and causes all the potential energy to collapse into an

> electron (matter). Thus, it manifests from a realm of infinite possibilities and unknown to a known. It becomes local in space and time."
>
> — *Dr. Joe Dispenza*
> *Becoming Supernatural*

To change your reality, you must shift your attention and focus it intentionally on a new concept of self.

You, as the awareness—the observer—are the one causing potential energy to collapse into form, from the realm of infinite possibilities to a known fact in your life.

You are not a passive participant. Your attention and observation determine the outcome.

If you want to change your facts or results, you must change your concept of yourself. You must assume the identity of the person who already thinks, feels, acts, and has what you Desire.

As Neville Goddard says in his book *The Power of Awareness*:

> "The events which you observe are determined by the concept you have of yourself. If you change the concept of yourself, the events ahead of you in time are altered. An assumption is a certain

> motion of consciousness. This motion, like all motion, exercises an influence on the surrounding substance, causing it to take the shape of, echo and reflect the assumption. A change of fortune is a new direction and outlook, merely a change in the arrangement of the same mind substance, consciousness. If you would change your life, you must begin at the very source with your own basic concept of self."

If we combine these two great resources, Neville Goddard and Dr. Joe Dispenza, we can understand more deeply how the quantum field—the realm of infinite possibilities—*is* that one substance of consciousness.

The awareness and attention you give to an idea or an assumption is what moves this one substance of consciousness and turns it into forms, conditions and events in your life. As David Bohm said in his book *Wholeness & The Implicate Order*:

> "In this flow, mind and matter are not separate substances. Rather they are different aspects of one whole and unbroken movement."

What quantum physics' research, with Heisenberg and Bonn's theories, shows us is that the mere observation—the conscious awareness—is what makes that possibility, which exists as a frequency or a wave, to collapse into matter.

The image you hold of yourself, that is programmed into your subconscious mind, shapes your reality. This is because your subconscious is inseparable with the universal mind, and therefore your self-concept moves the very substance of consciousness into its form.

The emotional and physical reality you currently experience reflects the possibilities you observe and accept. By observing a different possibility, accepting it as an undoubted assumption, and impressing this new concept upon your subconscious mind, you can create a new blueprint and manifest a new reality. We will explore these practices in more detail in subsequent chapters.

With the same repetition that once shaped your subconscious, while your brain was operating in Theta brainwaves in the first years of your life, you now have the power to create a new self-image and observe its potentiality turning into a fact. It takes practice. It is possible!

You are literally directing energy—the most potent force in every cell of your body- the infinite amount of information within you—into matter, based on your observation, and what you're giving your attention to.

Where attention is directed, energy flows and materializes.

If attention is given to limitations or past experiences that do not support new possibilities, the same patterns continue to manifest. Most people focus on what has been or what currently is, which prevents the creation of something new.

Energy collapses into matter based on observation. Without conscious control over attention, the ability to create desired outcomes is limited. This explains why many people remain stuck, unable to change their circumstances—they are not mastering their ability to direct attention and emotions.

> "Our control over things is part of the necessary order of the universe. The disorder we have met with in the past has resulted precisely from our never having attempted consciously to introduce this element of our personal control as part of the system...We may have taken a few steps on the way as yet, but they are in the right direction. And what we have to do now is to go on."
>
> — *Thomas Troward*
> *The Hidden Power*

To truly move energy with intention, you must understand the extraordinary system through which that energy flows—your Human Instrument.

In the next chapter, we'll explore this multidimensional vessel and how to align its full power with your Soul's Desire.

Integration

1. Identify one area of your life where you've been giving attention to what was or is, instead of what you desire to create.

2. Write a clear, present-tense assumption that expresses your new chosen concept of self in this area.
3. Support this process with the guided meditation available on **www.skilloffreedom.com**
4. Ask yourself: What does it feel like to become the observer who collapses this possibility into form?

(Optional) Record your new assumption and listen to it daily, reinforcing the direction of your attention.

11

THE HUMAN INSTRUMENT

"Bodies are vehicles of Consciousness."

—PAUL SELIG

Let's use the image of the river as a metaphor for life and this journey.

The river is the oneness that you are part of. The ship is your Instrument, your vehicle.

Who You Truly Are is an individuation of the whole: the water, the trees, the sky, the banks of the river—all of it. That is the Oneness you are part of. And that Oneness is always flowing in one direction: expansion, growth, creation.

Yet as a human, you can choose to steer with the current or against it. You can align with expansion, wellbeing, and natural evolution, or you can resist, contracting into disintegration and struggle.

You are always choosing: unity or separation. Increase or limitation.

As the master within you awakens, you become more skilled at navigating your ship, your Human Instrument, choosing to move with life, rather than against it.

Your Human Instrument is composed of three integrated parts: mind, heart, and body.

Let's explore each one.

The Mind

The mind is the *Wheel* of your Instrument, guiding the flow of energy through your attention. Where your attention goes, the energy of life follows. Ensure this wheel is guided by your conscious, present self, rather than your ingrained conditioning.

The mind is also the *Image Maker*. It forms the blueprint of your Desire, giving shape to unseen energy through vivid thought-forms that act as seeds of creation. These mental images are not just fantasies; they are frequencies that magnetize the elements needed to bring your vision into form.

The mind is also the *Projector*. Energy is moving to and through you, like light does through a projector, and whatever image you hold on the screen of your mind is then projected onto the screen of your life, your reality.

The mind is also the *Processor*. It receives and organizes information from your five physical senses. On a biological level, this processing happens through the brain, which is a physical expression of the mind—it is the mind in action.

The way you process information shapes your perception, and with repetition, these perceptions solidify into beliefs about yourself, others, and reality. These beliefs, in turn, form the framework of your personal experience. Your conscious mind gives you choice: you get to decide which ideas to consider, reject, accept or develop.

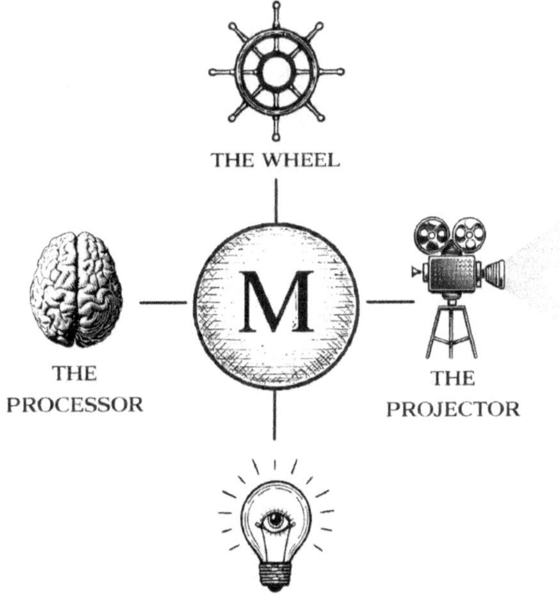

The Heart

The heart is the *Seat of your Soul*, a sacred bridge to the divine. It is the inner throne, the creative center of your Instrument, where your kingdom or queendom resides.

It is also the *Incubator*, where the spiritual seed—the divine idea or inspiration you've received—is planted. Once rooted in the soil of your subconscious, it grows, nurtured by your focused attention, until it manifests in physical form.

Your heart is also your *Sequencer*, the part of your Instrument in which the subconscious program resides. The program is a multitude of patterns and sequences of thoughts, beliefs, concepts, emotional reactions and habits that manifest in your physical reality.

Your heart is your *GPS*, the part of you that indicates the direction in which you are moving, whether wanted or unwanted. Your emotions are feedback. They tell you whether you're moving in alignment or off course.

Your mind is the wheel, directing your course. Your heart tells you whether you are moving in the right direction, towards the destination you've set for your journey.

Your emotions reflect your vibration, the frequency you're tuned into, shaped by the program running your internal operating system.

You are never disconnected from guidance. Your GPS is always on. You just have to listen.

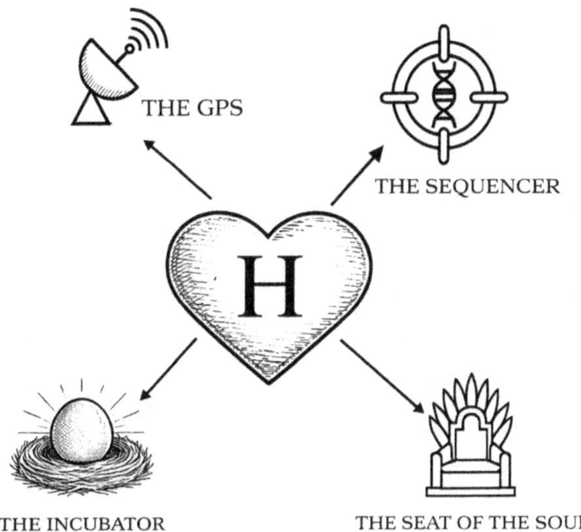

The Body

Your body is the *Vehicle* itself, the physical vessel moving through time and space. It is the part of your Instrument that acts, receives, and experiences.

If the mind is the wheel and the heart is the GPS, the body is the carrier itself.

Your body is the *Physical Expression* of your subconscious mind; it is your programming in motion. Your brain, your cells, your behaviour—all of it is shaped by what has been embedded and nurtured within your heart.

It's through the body that energy is expressed. It's through the body that spirit becomes matter. This is where the invisible becomes visible, where pure energy turns into form.

Your body acts as a *Receptor*, continually processing feedback from the physical world. Your senses collect impressions, and your nervous system interprets them, allowing you to experience the reality you've created.

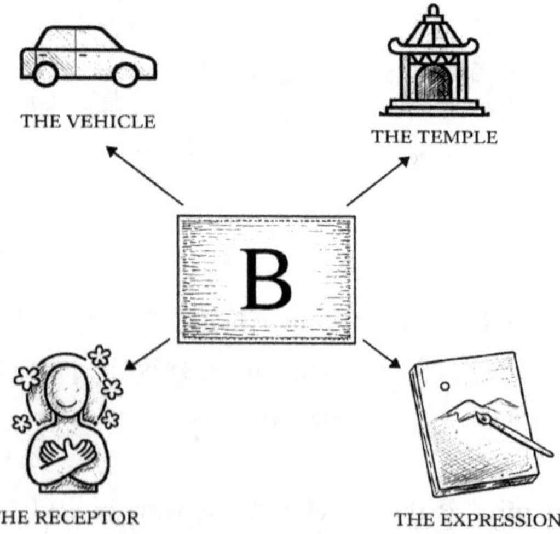

Your body is your *Temple*, the vessel through which Soul, Life, and Energy find expression. It is the Instrument through which you manifest your Desire and experience life on the physical plane.

The Integration of Mind, Heart, and Body

You are a spiritual being, pure consciousness, moving through a physical form.

Your mind directs, selects and processes. Your heart feels and guides. Your body moves, acts and experiences.

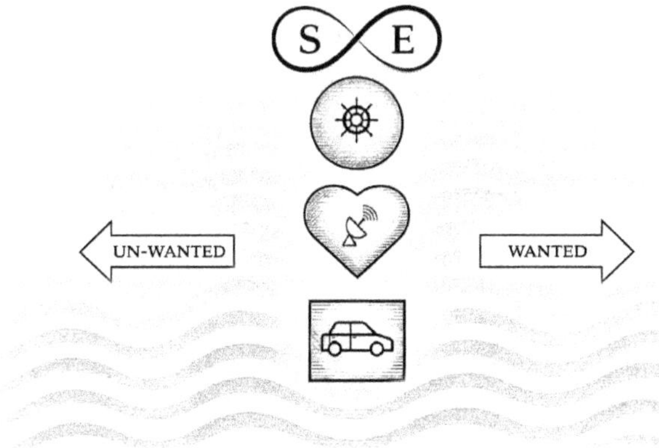

When aligned, they become a unified Instrument, capable of tuning into divine frequency and expressing it into physical reality.

This is the Human Instrument.
And you are its Master.

In the next chapter, we'll explore the multidimensional nature of your being and how your Human Instrument can access and shift timelines by aligning with the Eternal Now.

But first, take some time to integrate chapter 11 with a powerful meditation.

Integration

To deepen the alignment of your Human Instrument, support this process with the guided meditation available on **www.skilloffreedom.com**

This guided experience will support you in attuning the subtle frequencies of your being, so you can become a more coherent, resonant channel for your Soul's expression.

12

SHIFTING TIMELINES / THE MULTIDIMENSIONAL YOU

"The distinction between the past, present, and future is only a stubbornly persistent illusion."

—ALBERT EINSTEIN

Get ready to jump into the deeps:

Who You Truly Are is an infinitude expressed as a focal point on the leading edge of creation. The whole of creation exists in the Eternal Now. What we consider as past or future is a subjective perception, and not an absolute truth or reality.

To understand the deeper potential of time as a creative tool, let's briefly explore how modern physics reframes time itself:

In Newtonian physics, time is absolute. It ticks at the same rate for everyone, everywhere. But in Einstein's special relativity, time is relative to the point of observation or locality. According to his theory, space and time are not separate, but are interwoven to form a four-dimensional fabric called *Spacetime*. All points in time—past, present, and future—exist as coordinates within this four-dimensional continuum.

Just as every point in space exists regardless of where you are, every point in time exists regardless of *when* you are.

From this view, time doesn't flow. It's all there at once. We experience it sequentially only due to how our Instrument processes it according to its program's setting.

Think of a beam of white light passing through a prism. All the colors are already present, distinct yet unified in the light.

But your Human Instrument is tuned to focus on each hue separately, moving through the spectrum in a narrow, ordered way. To you, it seems like each color appears and then fades into the next. But in Truth, the full spectrum has always been there, only your perception moves, revealing one segment of light while the rest remain held in the whole.

What does that mean *for you?*

It means that you are multidimensional, and all other versions of yourself, on all infinitely possible timelines, exist *Now* and can be accessed by you with the right use of your Instrument, which has the capacity to tune into levels of vibration beyond those that have materialized into your current physical reality.

You can imagine your current timeline playing out on a horizontal plane—what we perceive as the linear past, present, and future. But there is also a vertical axis: the realm of the Eternal Now, where all possibilities already exist, waiting for you to tune in.

Everything in your current physical reality is a reflection of perceptions, thoughts, and emotions you've previously demonstrated.

The reality of what you experience as your future is accessible to you Now.

You can, when you master your Instrument and skill, shift timelines and move from the current to another of your choice.

The timeline you're living plays out on the horizontal plane of 3D reality. The Eternal Now exists on the vertical axis—the axis of infinite possibility and creative access.

Let's give an example:

Perhaps you've always identified as someone who struggles with money, having grown up with phrases like "we can't afford that" or witnessing others constantly striving just to get by. This past version of you learned to anticipate scarcity, make cautious choices, and settle for less.

However, an inner awakening occurs, connecting you to a version of yourself that understands how to manage wealth. This isn't just positive thinking; it's transforming into someone who elevates their standards.

You stop accepting undercharging for your time or service. You decline draining commitments. You invest with conscious consideration, not out of fear. You begin to communicate, act, and even navigate your day with the conviction that this abundant version is already real. This isn't pretense—it's alignment.

And this alignment starts to bridge the gap between your past self and a future where wealth is your lived experience.

3D, 4D and 5D

Here's the key. You are not only the old self or the new self. You are much more than that. You are a multidimensional being.

Just like an object has the three dimensions of length, width, and height, it also has the fourth dimension of time, because everything in the physical world exists over time.

Just like every dimension adds a quality to existence, the fourth dimension adds the quality of change.

Let me explain:

Look at this dot. It has zero dimensions.

•

0D (zero dimensions)

When the dot becomes a line, it receives the quality of length and has one dimension.

1D – length

When this line becomes a square, it receives the quality of width or height, and it now has two dimensions. It exists in two dimensions of length and height.

2D – length and height

When we add another dimension to it, it receives the quality of depth and now exists in three dimensions.

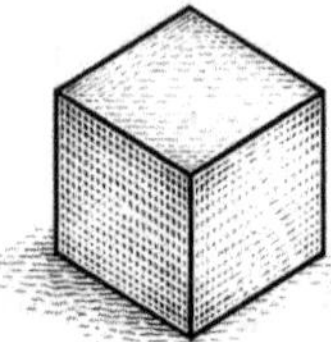

3D – length, height, and depth

When we add the fourth dimension of time, it receives the quality of *changeability.*

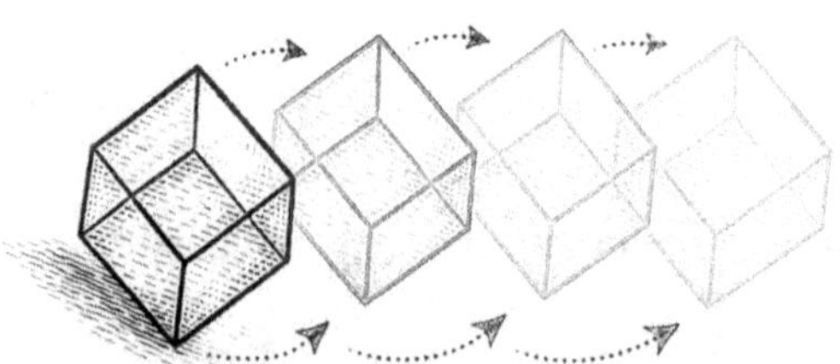

4D – change over time

When you bisect a three-dimensional object, you see its lower dimensions: a cube becomes a square, a square becomes a line.

This means that everything we perceive with our physical senses in physical reality is only a cross-section of a fourth-dimensional existence of the thing.

Everything exists in a constant state of flux and movement.

We only perceive it right here and now as a fixed reality in its fixed form. But when we are able to access with our awareness the fourth dimension of time, we can perceive more cross-sections and recognize the multidimensional reality.

And the same goes for *you*. What you perceive as yourself right now—your personality, your body and your personal reality—are just a cross-section of a multidimensional self that is in a constant state of change.

This means that in the Eternal Now, right now, with your Human Instrument, you can access any version of this ever-changing self that you are, and choose the cross-section that matches your vision, your Desire—the reality that you want to create for yourself—and embody that version of yourself right now.

All versions of you exist in the Eternal Now.

Imagine flipping through the pages of a flipbook. Each page is a moment, a version, a scene. When you look at just one page, you see a still image. But when you flip through the book, the motion—the life—comes to full view.

You are not just the page you're on. You are the whole book.

And when you master your Human Instrument, you can begin to turn the pages consciously, accessing other versions of you that already exist beyond this moment and bringing them into form.

Just like a place you know, that is located away from where you are, still exists and you can travel to it in order to experience it physically, so too does the version of yourself who is already living your Desire exists and can be accessed and experienced by you.

The travel is vibrational and is done in the Now, on the vertical axis of creation. That is how you access the fourth dimension and manifest its quality of change.

Linear vs. Eternal Time

Kronos and Kairos are two ancient Greek concepts of time that offer profoundly different understandings, one linear and quantitative, the other qualitative and experiential. Kronos (Chronos) refers to clock time—linear, measurable, and sequential.

Kairos is the sacred Divine Time, the Eternal Now.

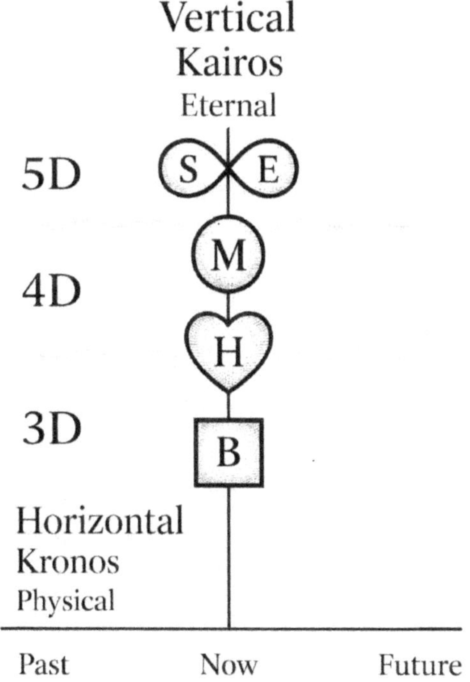

S—Spirit ; E—Energy ; M—Mind ; H—Heart ; B—Body

This ancient understanding of time, where Kairos refers to the deep, sacred Now, and Kronos to the unfolding of events, mirrors what both mystics and modern physicists describe as multidimensional time.

Imagine two intersecting lines forming a compass:

The horizontal line represents Kronos: the timeline you're walking, moment by moment, from past to future (3D).

The vertical line is Kairos: the axis of pure potential, the Eternal Now, where everything already exists in vibrational form. This is the door to the fifth dimension (5D)—the quantum field, the spiritual realm, the non-physical domain of infinite possibilities and creative access.

When your Human Instrument, mind, heart, and body, comes into coherence along the vertical axis, you gain access to the frequency of Who You Truly Are as a Divine Being.

In that state, you attune to the vibrational blueprint of your Desire, already existing in the non-physical realm (4D), not as something to reach for, but as a version of reality you can now embody.

And through that embodiment, what already exists beyond physical perception begins to materialize into form, which is what you experience as the unfolding of your future on the horizontal axis (3D).

This is the power you hold.

At any moment, you can shift timelines by mastering your Instrument, cracking the code of your current reality, and tuning yourself to a higher frequency. This alignment places you on a new horizontal plane, where your desired vision becomes the reality you live, as you embody a greater version of yourself.

Having explored the multidimensional nature of time, frequency, and the quantum field, we now return to the Human Instrument—to activate it.

In the next chapter, we'll uncover the six inner keys that grant you mastery over this sacred vessel, allowing you to consciously direct it from within.

Integration

Practice circulating energy and raising the frequency of your field with this intentional breathwork:

Close your eyes. As you inhale, breathe in from the vertical axis—drawing energy from Mother Earth and the higher realms.

As you exhale, send your breath out through the horizontal plane—sharing life, coherence, and presence with the world around you.

You can use this exercise in any physical environment or situation that brings negative or triggering influences. Instead of letting external vibrations affect your state, apply this breath with intention—even with your eyes open.

Let your awareness and Instrument transmute lower frequencies into higher ones.

To deepen your ability to shift timelines and bring all levels of your being into atonement, Support this process with the guided meditation available on **www.skilloffreedom.com**

13

KEYS TO MASTERY

"One can have no smaller or greater mastery than mastery of oneself."

—LEONARDO DA VINCI

*(*The framework of the six higher faculties presented in this chapter was received through the teachings of my late teacher, Bob Proctor, and is explored here through the author's own lived experience and practice.)*

Your Instrument has some very powerful and important features that enable you to communicate with the non-physical and unseen. It allows you to create thought-forms, move energy into those forms, and materialize them into your physical reality.

How extraordinary is that?

One of the most important keys to do that is your *Intuition.*

Intuition

It's called the sixth sense for a reason. Intuition is just as vital to your wellbeing as any of your five physical senses, and just as natural.

If you knew you could at any time call God Almighty and All-Knowing to ask for guidance and direction, wouldn't you?

Your intuition is your open line to God, to your Soul, to the Source of All.

Communication on this line is done through different means: feelings, synchronicities, dreams, and ideas, to name a few.

This vital communication flows through sundry streams: the whisper of feeling, the tapestry of synchronicity, the canvas of dreams, and the sudden spark of insight—to name a few. While some may literally hear words or messages, more often, this guidance comes through subtler means.

But every Human Instrument has Intuition and communicates with the Divine. What is most important is to follow the guidance received through your Key of Intuition with action!

This can be challenging, because you might be guided to take leaps of Faith, big or small, and count on the unseen forces to support you, trusting that the path to your Desire is and will continue unfolding.

It is important to have a very clear image of where you want your path to lead you. The key with which you create that image is your *Imagination*.

Imagination

With this key you can create literally anything.

Are you using your imagination to your favor, or the opposite?

If you often think about worst-case scenarios and what can go wrong, then you are using your powerful imagination against your own wellbeing.

What you dare to hold in your imagination, you will be able to hold in your hands, if you nourish it with Faith, feeling and action.

With your imagination, you create the form, and then you think and feel life into it. In other words, you tune into a frequency of a potentiality and then draw it to you by moving the energy with your attention and emotions.

So, wouldn't you agree that it is of the highest importance to master your Key of Imagination, so you actually tune into the potential future you desire, and not the one you dread?

The key that gives you the ability to keep holding the image you desire is your *Will.*

Will

This key gives you the ability to focus, and as the phrase goes, *what you focus on expands*. Another known phrase is, *where attention goes, energy flows*. Both affirm the same Truth: your Key of Will gives you the power to direct your attention and keep focus on the image of your desired future.

When we say *free will*, we actually mean the freedom to *choose* what to focus on. *This freedom is a skill you can practice and master*, and it is the *only* freedom there is. Any other form of freedom; financial freedom, time freedom, physical freedom—are all reflections of the one and only freedom: the freedom to choose what to think.

Understanding the universal laws and the principles of creation is essential is the doorway to freedom. The key that gives you the ability to think and understand is your *Reason*.

Reason

There is a great difference between reason and logic, although we often use these words interchangeably. Logic often reflects a set of beliefs shaped by culture and conditioning. What may seem logical at one point in time may seem illogical at another.

Reason is your ability to think and choose which concepts and ideas to accept and which to reject. You do not have to succumb to others' opinions or to worldwide views. You must stand guard at the gate of your mind and make sure that only the impressions that support your wellbeing and Desire are impressed onto the operating system of your Human Instrument.

Your Reason is the Key that opens or closes that gate, and it is vitally important that you practice and master it.

Another powerful key in your Instrument is *Perception.*

Perception

Napoleon Hill, in his legendary book *Think and Grow Rich,* shares how every time he had a problem or a challenge, he would mastermind in his imagination with some of the greatest minds he most admired, like Ralph Waldo Emerson, Thomas Edison, Henry Ford, Charles

Darwin and others. He would tap into their perspectives on the matter and would change his perception accordingly. And naturally, as his perception shifted, so did his experience.

Wayne Dyer said *"Change the way you look at things, and the things you look at change."*

As we discussed, the creative process is a cycle of Perception → Selection → Expression → Experience → Perception, and so on... This means that how you perceive your experience leads to a new selection you then make of how you desire to express and then experience life.

In this perpetual, never-ending process, there is an infinite number of perspectives you can choose from on any matter.

The Law of Polarity decrees that everything has its equal opposite. This means that if you experience something as difficult, there is an equal level of ease accessible for you. The key of Perception is the one that opens that door and gives you access to the opposite positive pole.

You must train yourself to use your Human Instrument so that you can harness this ability to define your perception in a way that supports and perpetuates your wellbeing (and the wellbeing of others), and not vice versa. Most of us misuse or even abuse our Human Instrument and these keys in self-sabotaging ways.

Let's look into another key that is mostly misused in such a way: *Memory.*

Memory

How often do you use your memory to recall joy, success, or moments of lightness—on purpose?

Most people ruminate mostly on past trauma, disappointments, and mistakes, playing over and over those memories in their mind, and by that, copy-pasting that past onto their future.

You can train yourself to use your Key of Memory and tap into recollections that ignite the feeling of what you desire to manifest, even if those are of unrelated past events.

For example, you can recall the first time you rode your bicycle all by yourself, or managed to ski down a hill freely, or when you received a gift and felt appreciated, grateful, and happy. In doing so, you use the Key of Memory to unlock those emotions, and by that, to move the energy in the direction of your Desire, by tuning into its frequency.

You can also use this key to create memories from your future. Your brain and subconscious mind do not know the difference between events that actually occurred physically and those you "only" imagine. Research shows that when you mentally rehearse a future or imagined event or actions, your brain changes to look like the event has already happened.

When visualizing the desired future, you are literally creating a memory that is physically registered in the neurocircuitry of your brain, just like memories of past events do.

So when we say, *"you must become the person living the future you desire,"* it's not just poetic—it's biological. You can, and must, change your biology to match that 'grandest version of the greatest vision' of who you desire and are called to be.

You can practice and master your Human Instrument to do this. Remember, we are talking about a skill which requires practice. So even if you don't feel like you can choose where to focus, or how to receive divine guidance and follow it, or how to visualize your Desire and believe in its certainty, or how to shift perspectives and accept only concepts that support your Desire, even if they contradict your logic—these are all skills that you can practice and master!

Mastery is the result of devoted practice. In the next chapter we'll look into the daily essentials for this practice, so you can **crack the code of your Human Instrument and master the Skill of Freedom!**

Integration

Each of the keys in your Human Instrument is a skill you can train. Choose one to focus on for the next few days—or cycle through all six, one per day, as a devotional practice.

These are not traits you either have or don't have. They're muscles. Use them consciously, and they grow stronger. Mastery begins and sustains in practice.

Intuition

Practice: Pause before making a decision—big or small. Place your hand on your heart, take one breath, and ask: *What does Truth feel like here?*

Imagination

Practice: Spend 3 minutes visualizing a desired future outcome. See it, feel it, and stay with it as if it's already physically real.

Will

Practice: Choose one thought, image, or intention—and hold your attention on it for 2 uninterrupted minutes. If the mind wanders, gently return.

Reason

Practice: Notice one belief or idea that doesn't serve your expansion. Question it. Ask: *Do I have to keep this? Is there something truer I can choose?*

Perception

Practice: When faced with a challenge, ask yourself: *What's another way to see this? What's the hidden opportunity or gift here?*

Memory

Practice: Recall a past moment of joy, empowerment, or clarity. Let that memory flood your system with its original feeling. Then hold your vision for the future from *that* frequency.

14

THE ESSENTIALS: FOUR PILLARS OF EMBODIMENT

"Persistence is to the character of man what carbon is to steel."

—NAPOLEON HILL

Developing a skill and mastering an instrument requires practice. Skills, habits, and patterns are created through consistent and frequent repetition.

Whatever you think, feel, and do frequently sets your *frequency.*

There are a few components to this practice which, if persisted in, will develop your mastery of your Human Instrument and the Skill of Freedom.

1. Meditation

The purpose and effect of the meditation practice have a few layers.

Accessing the Field

First and foremost, it is in the meditative state that you have access to the Eternal Now, which exists in the present moment, and to the non-physical unified field where all possibilities exist.

Everything you desire and don't yet have in your physical reality exists as a potentiality or frequency, in the non-physical, unified field. This field can be called The Unknown because it remains unmanifested in your material experience. You can bring this potentiality into physical reality by accessing this field with your own Instrument and, through the creative process, bring that potentiality into manifested physical reality.

Outside of meditation, your mind often operates in survival mode, constantly scanning the external world, interpreting it through past experiences. In that state, even when you think about the future, you're usually doing it through the lens of the familiar past. You're not imagining something new, but rehearsing variations of what you've already lived.

This is how the survival mind tries to protect you: by predicting what's next based on what's already known. But it's also how it limits you, keeping your attention trapped in the past, and your energy anchored to an old timeline.

Most of the time, your attention is consumed by what you see, hear, and experience physically. As a result, you're operating in the known, recycling the past, and projecting it onto the future.

To tap into the unknown and shape a new future, you must be fully present in the current moment. Accessing this presence requires shifting your focus from the familiar past and anticipated future, where your mind typically resides, and truly immersing yourself in the Now.

Through meditation, you can practice directing your attention to the present, the Eternal Now, the unified field, and the potential you wish to manifest.

In meditation, you also connect with The Truth of Who You Are, to your Soul, and to the Divine that is within, and all around you.

We live in a culture and era that is oriented to mental and mechanical models of thought and operation and, for the most part, disregards any deity. By this model, the analytical mind is the leading faculty rather than the Heart. But the Heart is the seat of your Soul and your door to the Divine.

You are not alone on this journey. You've got God / The Universe on your side. The more you are aware of its presence and connect to it, the more aware you are of its power and love, the more you are empowered and able to receive and direct it.

> "Spirit awaits direction from the soul."
> — *John Wesle*

Heart-Brain Coherence

One of the meanings of the word Heart, as we often use it, is *center.* We say *the heart of the city, the heart of the team*, etc. Indeed, the Heart is the primary factor of matter.

Dr. Joe Dispenza calls the Heart our *creative center* and explains that our Heart is electric, and when beating coherently, it generates an energy field that expands up to three meters wide and transmits information.

We know that the Heart sends signals to the brain, that have a significant effect on the brain's function. When the Heart is in coherence, these signals are improving the nervous system, hormonal balance, and even gene expression.

You bring your Heart into coherence by cultivating elevated emotions while regulating the heartbeat.

In meditation, you are able to direct your breath and slow down your heartbeat, while focusing in a way that can elevate your emotions and create this Heart-Brain

Coherence, which in turn affects your body, as well as the unified field.

Activating The Pineal Gland

You can also learn how to direct your breath in a way that activates your Pineal Gland. Your pineal gland is, in fact, what is considered your third eye, which is another energetic center in your body and field that sends and receives signals.

In your pineal gland, there are very small crystals which, when activated, function literally like radio antennas. By directing your breath in a certain way, especially in a meditative state, you are able to move the cerebral fluid in your spine to push against the pineal gland and mechanically activate those crystals. The ancient yogis knew about this thousands of years ago, and Dr. Joe Dispenza teaches this technique and practice as a central methodology.

Mental Rehearsal

Meditation can also be applied for Mental Rehearsal. Research shows that the brain doesn't know the difference between an experience that is, or has physically occurred, and an experience created in imagination.

For example, in a groundbreaking study at Harvard Medical School, neuroscientist Dr. Alvaro Pascual-Leone demonstrated that mental rehearsal can physically alter the brain. Two groups of participants were taught a simple five-finger piano exercise: one group physically practiced for five days, while the other only imagined playing the piece, visualizing each finger movement without touching the keyboard. Brain scans using transcranial magnetic stimulation revealed that both groups showed nearly identical changes in the motor cortex—the part of the brain responsible for finger movement.

This study offered compelling evidence that the brain can rewire itself through pure thought, underscoring the power of intentional mental practice.

This means that in a meditative state, you are able to change your brain circuitry to be wired as if the events you desire to experience have already happened. This also means that in this meditative practice, you are literally and neurologically becoming that version of yourself who is living that reality you desire to create, which will naturally lead you to behave, make decisions and access the possibilities available to that version of yourself.

You can now see and understand how thoughts do, in fact, turn into things—into neurological circuits in your brain!

Resetting Your Inner Frequency

One more aspect to the meditative state is the altering of the brainwaves. Remember what we said about the reprogramming process and how in the early years of your life, your brain was operating on Theta brainwaves, which made you completely suggestible to all impressions, concepts, and ideas?

By mentally rehearsing in this receptive state in meditation, the images and emotions you intentionally generate are received directly by your subconscious, updating your inner programming to match the frequency of your desired future.

You literally create your own destiny.

I trust that you can see now how meditation is an essential part of the practice and mastery of your Human Instrument.

2. Autosuggestion

Another aspect of the initial programming process you Human Instrument underwent in your early life is repetition. The impressions you received from your environment were repeated, through words, reactions, emotional patterns and so on, and gradually became internalized as your own recurring thoughts, feelings, and behaviors.

Over time, these repeated experiences formed well-worn pathways in the brain—neural circuits that began to fire automatically, without conscious intention.

It's like walking the same path through a field every day. Eventually, the grass lays flat, and a visible trail forms.

Your mind works the same way. What you repeat becomes the default route. And those automatic thoughts continue to shape your reality through the creative process, whether you're aware of them or not.

Studies show that most of the thoughts you think in a day are the same as in the day before. In his research, psychologist Eric Klinger found that up to 98% of daily thoughts may be habitual or repetitive in nature.

Thought is one of the core operations of your Human Instrument, and so it's vital that you gain freedom, choice, and precision in your thinking.

Through the autosuggestion practice you craft thoughts that match your desired state of being and deliberately repeat them on a continuous basis. Through this practice you override the old, outdated patterns and create new ones, that will eventually become automatic.

When you stop feeding an old thought, the neural pathway weakens and begins to dissolve, like a trail that disappears when no one walks it. In like manner, when you repeat a new thought, you establish a new neurological network.

This process is supported by neuroscience research on synaptic pruning, which shows that neural pathways strengthen with use and fade with neglect, allowing the brain to continuously rewire itself based on focus and repetition.

In 1949, Canadian neuropsychologist Donald Hebb proposed a groundbreaking theory about how the brain learns and adapts. Known as "Hebb's Rule" it states: *"Neurons that fire together, wire together."*

This principle suggests that when two neurons activate simultaneously, the connection between them strengthens. Over time, repeated activation of the same neural pathways leads to more efficient communication between neurons, laying the neurological foundation for learning, memory, and habit formation.

While Hebb focused on the strengthening of neural connections, later research uncovered a complementary process: synaptic pruning. Neuroscientist Peter Huttenlocher was one of the first to show that in early childhood, the brain produces an overabundance of synaptic connections and then selectively eliminates the less-used ones during adolescence and early adulthood.

Together, Hebbian theory and synaptic pruning offer a powerful lens through which to understand how mental focus, repetition, and experience shape the architecture of the brain, reinforcing what is practiced, and clearing out what is neglected.

The Mind and the Body are parts of your Human Instrument. You can also refer to them as Conscious and Subconscious, because the body is 100% a reflection or representation of the subconscious, as everything else in your physical experience is. Through deliberate use of the conscious part of the Instrument, you are able to shift and update its subconscious programming, which in turn changes the brain, body and the physical experience.

3. Study

Understanding this process and the laws by which it operates is vital. True understanding is a deep acceptance and integration of knowledge. You may already believe these concepts mentally, but real transformation happens when they take root in your subconscious, not just your intellect.

In order to change your physical reality, you must truly understand. Information alone does not create transformation. It is the integration of the information that leads to change.

Bob Proctor used to say, *"Faith based on understanding is the key to freedom."*

In order to master the Skill of Freedom, and deliberately create desired experiences with your Human Instrument, you must see beyond what has already manifested physically and believe in what is yet unseen. That is Faith. It is a skill. And skills, as we know, are developed and maintained through repetition.

Studying these concepts, laws and truths continuously and consistently, repeating over and over again the same segments, resources and lessons, is an essential part of the daily practice of the Skill of Freedom.

4. Tuning

Directing your thoughts deliberately is crucial. But if you want to crack the code of your Human Instrument, you must practice your ability to change your mood.

Emotional freedom is the one and only true freedom there is.

Emotions are energy in motion. Everything is made of energy. Whatever the change you want to create and experience, it will come about only through a change in the movement of energy. Your Human Instrument directs that movement.

How do you know in which direction the energy is moving through your Instrument? By the way you feel! And if you want to move the energy deliberately, then you must practice your ability to do so.

Your emotional system is incredibly valuable and central to your being. It forms a direct link to your Soul, enabling you to navigate the unseen and receive information and guidance from your Soul's higher intelligence and awareness.

It is essential that you practice your ability to tune your Instrument to the frequencies that match your Soul's Desire. When you feel negative emotions, you are basically receiving signals from your emotional GPS system that you are moving in the opposite direction of your desired destination. When you are feeling positive emotions, you are in fact in resonance with your Soul and are moving in the desired direction.

You might be thinking: *but how can I change the way I feel?*

Well, once again, that is a skill! Which means that with practice, you can master your mood.

To be clear, I'm not suggesting that negative emotions are wrong or that they should be suppressed. Quite the opposite, in fact! Without the capacity to feel negative emotions, your emotional guidance system would be dysfunctional.

It is a vital part of the Human Instrument to feel pain. If you couldn't feel physical pain, you wouldn't have known, for example, that your hand is touching the burning stove and could not have protected yourself from getting hurt.

And in like manner, your capacity to feel emotional pain allows you to protect and elevate your wellbeing.

It's not about avoiding negative emotions, but about the length of time it takes you to transmute the energy and tune your Instrument to a higher frequency. Some people stay stuck in an emotional reaction that lasts years and decades, reliving the pain, anger, or guilt of a traumatic event, and thus perpetuating the experience.

And so, it is vitally important that your daily practice includes developing and maintaining your ability to shorten the time span of negative emotions, using them as feedback that alerts you to the fact that you are engaging in thoughts and directing attention to what is not serving your wellbeing, and choose new thoughts that tune your frequency higher.

An essential way to tune your frequency is through your **Exit Points**. These are certain activities that will rapidly raise your frequency and help you make better choices of thoughts and feelings. This practice is especially important to use when there is already a momentous downward spiral and you realize you are way off your royal path.

Gratitude, for example, is a powerful practice for tuning your frequency. By deliberately directing your attention to what you have and appreciate, you can raise your frequency and shift the emotional energy you are experiencing.

The feeling of *Having* is the opposite of the feeling of *lack*, and therefore it is a frequency that matches your Desire, which you can tune to by dedicating some time every day to gently and firmly focusing on those things, people, conditions, and experiences you love and enjoy.

Other activities that may raise your frequency and serve as *exit points* may be physical movement, music, being in nature and more. It is essential to know your exit points, so when you are on a downward spiral, and are less inspired and motivated, you can easily recall and choose an activity that will pull you out of that trajectory and build a positive energetic momentum.

Take some time to write your exit points down ahead of time, like **a playlist for your emotional recalibration**. Your exit points are physical actions or environments that quickly uplift you and shift your energy in a positive way.

It may seem obvious to understand what brings you joy, but having a written list of exit points is crucial. This list will prepare you for when a downward spiral begins. When you're overwhelmed, anxious, or frustrated, your mind won't easily generate solutions to shift your state. However, with your exit points clearly defined, you can quickly choose one and redirect your path from an undesirable state to a desirable one.

Let's recap the essential elements of the practice that allow you to develop true mastery of the Human Instrument:

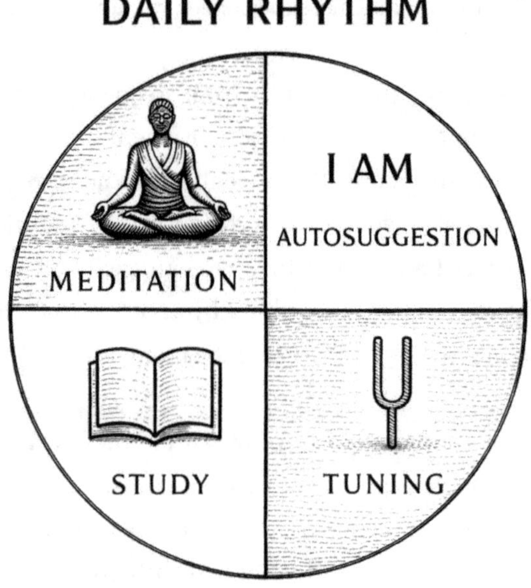

If you want to develop your Skill of Freedom, your daily practice must include the following four core components:

1. Meditation – The gateway to the Eternal Now and the unified field of all possibilities. Meditation allows you to access potential realities, connect with your Soul and the Divine, elevate your emotional state, create heart-brain coherence, activate your pineal gland, and rewire your brain through mental rehearsal.

2. Autosuggestion - Through deliberate repetition of thoughts aligned with your desired state of being, you override old patterns and establish new ones. This practice leverages the brain's natural capacity for neuroplasticity. With awareness and consistency, you transform your subconscious programming, and thus—your reality.

3. Study - True transformation requires integration, not just information. Repetition and immersion in universal truths cultivate Faith based on understanding, which is the key to freedom. Consistent daily study of these universal laws and principles helps you embody knowledge at the subconscious level so it becomes who you are, not just what you know.

4. Tuning - Your emotions reflect your frequency. To master your Instrument, you must learn to tune your emotional state. This includes recognizing emotional signals, shortening the time span of negative states, and accessing elevated emotions through your exit points, which are physical actions and environments that shift your energy quickly and reliably.

With the essentials in place, the path to your Desire unfolds.

Next, we'll learn how to read the road signs that guide and reflect your journey, so you can reach your desired destination.

Integration

Choose one of the four essentials: Meditation, Autosuggestion, Study, or Tuning and commit to practicing it daily for the next 7 days. If you're ready, build a simple daily rhythm that includes all four, or stack them up gradually, adding one more to your daily practice every 7 days.

Here's a template you can use or adapt:

Morning:

1. *5–10 minutes of meditation*
2. *Write down 5-10 things you appreciate having in your life.*
3. *Repeat your autosuggestion statements aloud*

Midday:

Tune your frequency by taking a conscious exit point break (e.g., nature, music, movement, beauty, gratitude)

Evening:

1. *Study one paragraph or page that reconnects you to your power*
2. *Reflect on what you practiced, what shifted, what you noticed*
3. *End the day with a short meditation.*

You don't have to do it all at once. You just have to begin. This is how you master your Instrument day by day, choice by choice.

15

ROAD SIGNS: FEEDBACK FROM REALITY

"Success is a progressive realisation of a worthy ideal."

—EARL NIGHTINGALE

As you guide your life's journey towards your Destin(y) ation, your innate emotional GPS and external signs along the way will provide directions and indications of your progress, showing your current position in relation to your desired future.

Every aspect of your current experience—your physical wellbeing, relationships, finances, career, and all other conditions and circumstances—serves as a road sign reflecting your present sequel.

These outcomes serve as crucial guides for conscious adjustments, revealing not just current actions but also the underlying subconscious patterns and beliefs that fuel them.

When something in your life isn't unfolding the way you'd hoped, it's simply a road sign showing you your current position on the path, how far you may be from your desired destination, or whether you've veered off course of your royal path.

Road signs aren't there to discourage you—they're there to guide you.

Without this essential awareness and understanding, you risk reacting emotionally to these signals, as most people often do. Instead of simply accepting the neutral and useful data, you might find yourself losing focus, Faith, and excitement, leading to frustration, worry, or anxiety.

Imagine driving to a desired, unfamiliar destination. After some time, you see a sign indicating either a long journey ahead or that you've made a wrong turn.

What would you do with that information?

Would you adjust your course and keep driving toward your destination? Or would you pull over, sit beneath the sign, and spiral into frustration or doubt?

Can you see the analogy here?

You must understand and operate in awareness of the universal Law of Cause and Effect.

When you let external conditions shape how you think, feel, and act, they become the cause—and then they perpetuate.

You must understand and remember that those incidents are—*incidental*. Your state of being is what's essential in the creative process. Do not mix these two up!

Operating in discord with the universal Law of Cause and Effect is detrimental to your wellbeing.

Would you jump off a high building window? Of course not, because you understand the law of gravity and would not operate in discord with it.

In like manner, operating in discord with the universal Law of Cause and Effect will harm you.

You must reframe how you perceive these road signs and the meaning you attach to them.

When a rocket is launched toward its target, it doesn't move in a perfect straight line. It constantly receives negative feedback and signals about where it's off-course and adjusts its course accordingly. Without these corrections, it could never reach its destination.

Can you see the analogy now?

Your results give you feedback, and when they do not match your Desire and goal, you are receiving essential negative signals, without which you can never find the right path and arrive at your destination.

It is your perception and emotional reaction that can, and must, change.

The trick is to be completely devoted to your goal—like a rocket locked onto its destination—while remaining unconcerned and completely detached from the immediate outcomes. Stay open to adjustments and don't be swayed by temporary deviations.

That's the sweet spot! That's the skill you want to master. That is how you free yourself from emotional bondage and lead yourself from within.

The journey itself is our true destination. If it were not, we would never set out on adventures, only to return home. Instead, we would remain there, ensnared by the illusion of comfort and security.

Remember, your success isn't measured by when you reach your destination, but by how you lead yourself along the way.

Integration

Choose one current result in your life that feels unwanted or uncomfortable—something external (money, health, time, relationship, etc.).

Ask yourself:

- What does this "road sign" reveal about my current course?
- What feedback is it offering without judgment or drama?
- How can I gently course-correct without falling into emotion or resistance?

Then, visualize your goal. Hold it in your awareness with love and commitment.

Now, imagine yourself *unhooking* from your current result—seeing it, but not absorbing it.

Repeat to yourself:

"This is useful feedback. I'm on my way."

Practice holding your Desire and releasing the meaning you've attached to the momentary result.

16

THE THRESHOLD

"We shall not cease from exploration, and the end of all our exploring will be to arrive where we started and know the place for the first time."

—T. S ELIOT

This is the quiet edge between structure and spirit.

Between everything you are practicing and the part of you that has always known.

The threshold isn't a destination. It's a shift in orientation.

Where method gives way to presence. Where what you once rehearsed becomes how you move.

This is where the work stops feeling like work. Where discipline is no longer effort, but a natural rhythm. Not something to carry, but something that carries you.

You don't need to memorise the steps anymore. They are already pulsing through your system, expressed through the way you walk, speak, choose and create.

You've studied the Human Instrument, its architecture of mind, heart, and body and the way it translates energy into form.

You've come to recognize how subconscious programming was formed and how it continues to shape experience. You've uncovered the mechanisms of thought, emotion, and perception that once ran on autopilot, and learned to direct them with awareness and choice

You've examined how the inner world projects onto the outer, and how attention, emotion, and belief interact to generate reality.

You've come to see time not as a fixed line, but as a dimensional field, and yourself as a multidimensional being.

You've discovered how Desire speaks in frequency, and how results reflect alignment and identity.

You've remembered that you are not a passive observer of life, but a participant in the unfolding of reality, working in harmony with the very laws that shape it.

And you've come to recognize the path, not as something to strive for, but as something you are already walking, step by step, with increasing clarity and trust.

There is no finish line.

This is the deeper current beneath the practice, a new way of being.

This is the threshold.

Integration

1. **Revisit what resonated**
   Go back through the notes, highlights, or reflections you captured while reading. Let yourself re-encounter the insights that struck a chord, challenged a pattern, or stirred something deeper.

2. **Re-enter the work**
   Choose one chapter, or one concept, that feels especially alive or relevant right now. Read it again, not as a beginner, but as someone who has walked further into the work. Let it meet you where you are now.

3. **Recognize what's ready to shift**
   Ask yourself: What Truth am I ready to embody more fully? What understanding am I now prepared to live? Notice what feels aligned to deepen into.

4. **Choose your focus**
   Select one practice, principle, or approach from the

book to carry with you intentionally for the next 30 days. Keep it simple and consistent. Let it anchor the next layer of integration.

5. **Declare your direction**
   Write a sentence that captures the essence of the path you are choosing now. Let it reflect the standard you are honoring, the awareness you are living, or the energy you are embodying.

6. **Keep it close**
   Place this sentence somewhere visible—on your mirror, in your journal, on your phone. Let it walk with you. Let it remind you that mastery is not a finish line. It's a way of being.

And when you return to these pages, as you inevitably will, notice what meets you differently. The path keeps unfolding. The Instrument keeps tuning.

17

I REMEMBER WHO YOU ARE IN TRUTH

"We may have taken only a few steps on the way as yet, but they are in the right direction, and what we have to do now is to go on."

—THOMAS TROWARD

You have arrived at this moment, dear one.

You now know Who You Are in Truth: a Divine being, an individuation of the Oneness, a Soul directing Spirit into form.

You are both the Creator and the creation, the artist and the masterpiece.

You are both the receiver and the Gift, the beloved and Love itself.

You now have the knowledge and the tools to turn Desire into experience, and experience into wisdom.

Keep going, dear one. Keep unraveling the Truth of Who You Are, opening new gates, and shining more of your beautiful Light.

Keep on rising to higher and higher levels of vibration and expression, inspiring all that is around you in this infinite collective process of creation.

Use this book as a manual to your Human Instrument and the Skill of Freedom, as you lead your path of evolution.

And if you ever forget, come back here and re-call.
Then, once again, answer the calling.

Let this book serve as your sacred re-minder.

It is my promise to you that I will always remember Who You Are in Truth.

Now walk your path, and light the way for others.

To your freedom, with love,
Shimrit Nativ
(The Little Keeper Of The Path)

GLOSSARY OF TERMS

Key concepts, metaphors, and teachings used throughout the book

The Human Instrument

Your body, mind, heart, and energetic system—an integrated vessel through which your Soul expresses, creates, and experiences life in the physical dimension. With understanding and practice, it becomes the most powerful tool for transformation, creation, and embodiment.

Desire

The voice of your Soul, calling you toward your purpose and potential. Not to be confused with need, which arises from lack. Desire is life-giving and expansive—it reveals your highest path.

The Wall of Separation

A symbolic barrier formed through conditioning and life experience that create the illusion of separation between the Human Self and the Divine Self. Gates in the wall open as lessons are learned and emotional patterns released.

Gates

Points of opportunity for growth and reconnection to your True Self. Each gate holds a lesson that, once integrated, allows more Divine light to flow through your Human Instrument.

Lessons

Transformational challenges encoded into recurring patterns. Each lesson offers the potential to transmute pain into wisdom and reclaim a deeper expression of Truth and richer experience of life.

The Royal Path

The Soul-aligned trajectory of your life—the path of Truth, freedom, expansion, and divine purpose. Your Soul knows this path, and your Human Instrument can be attuned to follow it.

The Spiral Path

The unfolding journey of growth, healing, and remembrance—where you revisit familiar patterns from deeper levels of awareness and embodiment each time.

The Primal Wound

The original imprint of separation, formed early in life, that sits at the base of the spiral path. It disconnects you from the Truth of Who You Are and creates core beliefs about love, safety, or worth needing to be earned. Healing it initiates deep transformation and return to wholeness.

Upper Limit
A concept introduced by Gay Hendricks in *The Big Leap*. It refers to a subconscious threshold on how much love, success, joy, or freedom a person allows themselves to experience. When this limit is exceeded, self-sabotaging behaviors often arise to restore familiar conditions. The Upper Limit is rooted in early subconscious programming and can be shifted through awareness and intentional reprogramming.

The Operating System
The subconscious patterns, beliefs, emotional responses, and behaviors that run automatically through your Human Instrument.

Emotional GPS
Your emotional guidance system, which reveals whether you're in or out of alignment with your Soul and desired reality. It gives you moment-by-moment feedback on the direction you are stirring your Human Instrument—in the wanted direction that leads to your desired future, or the opposite unwanted trajectory.

Frequency
The rate at which energy vibrates. Everything in existence—thoughts, emotions, objects, and experiences—has a frequency. Your Human Instrument continuously broadcasts and receives frequencies based on your thoughts, feelings, and actions. By aligning with the frequency of your desired reality, you draw it into form through the creative process.

The Unknown
The realm of unmanifested potential—everything that has not yet collapsed into physical form. It is accessed through Faith, imagination, and the present moment.

Faith
More than belief—it is a vibrational state and a deep knowing. Faith is the spiritual substance of the unseen, the energetic certainty of what is not yet manifested. It is the bridge between idea and reality, and the core of conscious creation.

Psychocybernetic Mechanism
A term coined by Dr. Maxwell Maltz. Describes the self-correcting inner system that returns you to your subconscious "settings"—until they are updated consciously.

Crystallized Goals

Clearly defined steps or destinations on the way to your greater vision. These goals provide focus, momentum, and energetic alignment with your Soul's path.

Tuning

The conscious practice of shifting your emotional state, frequency, and energetic field to match the vibration of your desired reality.

Exit Points

Actions, environments, or rituals that help you quickly shift your energy out of negative patterns and back into alignment. Essential tools for emotional tuning.

The Creative Process

The continuous cycle of perceiving → selecting → expressing → experiencing. Your Human Instrument shapes reality through this cycle—consciously or unconsciously.

The Grandest Version of the Greatest Vision of Who You Are

Origin: Neale Donald Walsch, *Conversations with God*

This phrase expresses the Soul's highest potential and calling. It refers to the ultimate Truth and divine possibility within you—the fullest, most loving, creative, and powerful expression of your being.

In this book, it serves as a guiding north star: an invitation to align your thoughts, emotions, and actions with the deeper knowing of Who You Truly Are, and to embody that Truth in every area of your life.

It is a reminder that you are both the artist and the masterpiece—and that your life is a sacred act of conscious creation.

BIBLIOGRAPHY

Allen, J. (1902). *As a Man Thinketh*. Thomas Y. Crowell & Co.

Calaprice, A. (Ed.). (2011). *The Ultimate Quotable Einstein*. Princeton University Press.

Dispenza, J. (2012). *Breaking the Habit of Being Yourself: How to Lose Your Mind and Create a New One*. Hay House.

Dyer, W. (1999). *Wisdom of the Ages: 60 Days to Enlightenment*. HarperCollins.

Einstein, A. (1920). *Relativity: The Special and the General Theory* (R. W. Lawson, Trans.). New York: Henry Holt and Company.

Einstein, A. (1955). Letter to the family of Michele Besso, March 1955. In A. Calaprice (Ed.), *The Ultimate Quotable Einstein* (p. 5). Princeton University Press.

Hendricks, G. (2009). *The Big Leap: Conquer Your Hidden Fear and Take Life to the Next Level*. HarperOne.

Hebb, D. O. (1949). *The Organization of Behavior: A Neuropsychological Theory*. New York: Wiley.

Hill, N. (1937). *Think and Grow Rich*. The Ralston Society.

Huttenlocher, P. R. (1979). Synaptic density in human frontal cortex—developmental changes and effects of aging. *Brain Research*, 163(2), 195–205.

Klinger, E. (1990). *Daydreaming*. Los Angeles, CA: Jeremy P. Tarcher, Inc.

Lao Tzu. (6th Century BCE). *Tao Te Ching* (Various translations used).

Maltz, M. (1960). *Psycho-Cybernetics: A New Way to Get More Living Out of Life*. Prentice Hall.

Minkowski, H. (1908). Space and Time. In H. A. Lorentz, A. Einstein, H. Minkowski, & H. Weyl, *The Principle of Relativity* (W. Perrett & G. B. Jeffery, Trans., 1923). New York: Dover Publications, 1952.

Nightingale, E. (1956). *The Strangest Secret*. Nightingale-Conant.

Proctor, B. (2008). *You Were Born Rich*. LifeSuccess Productions.

Selig, P. (2010). *I Am the Word: A Guide to the Consciousness of Man's Self in a Transitioning Time.* TarcherPerigee.

Tillich, P. (1963). Theological Dimensions of Time. In *The Protestant Era* (pp. 54–66). University of Chicago Press.

Troward, T. (1909). *The Creative Process in the Individual.* Robert Macoy Publishing.

Wallace, W. D. (1910). *The Science of Getting Rich.* Elizabeth Towne Company.

Eliot, T.S. (1943). Four Quartets. Harcourt.

Walsch, N. D. (1995). *Conversations with God, Book 1: An Uncommon Dialogue.* Putnam.

www.ingramcontent.com/pod-product-compliance
Lightning Source LLC
LaVergne TN
LVHW010702110826
845149LV00014B/3188

* 9 7 8 3 9 8 2 8 4 5 1 0 4 *